Law of States:
Domestic Affairs

Law of States:
Domestic Affairs

Taz Riot

Edited by: Collin Costa

Freeport
2018

Copyright

First Printing: 2018

ISBN: 978-0-359-08759-4

Freeport
1941 California Ave, Unit 77611
Corona, CA 92877

www.TazRiot.com

Dedication

To Dean Orton for helping me become the man I am today. A amazing friend, Doctor and moral compus.

To Mildred Hayden for the amazing lessons you have taught me over the years. For all the love and support you have given.

Contents

Taz Riot

Chapter 1: Sovereign States

A state is a body politic, a society of men united together for promoting and protecting their mutual safety and advantage by their combined strength.

The very design that includes a member of men to come together and form a society which has common interest, and which is to act as one. It is necessary that there shall be an established public authority, to order and direct what is to be done by each in relation to the end of the association. This political authority is the sovereignty, and he who are invested with it, are the sovereign.

It is evident that, by the very act of civil or political bounds, each citizen subjects themselves to the authority of the body politic. The authority of all over each member, therefore essentially belongs to the state. But the exercise of that authority may be placed in different hands, according as to the body politic may have ordained.

Every state which governs itself without dependence on any foreign power, is a sovereign state. Its rights are naturally the same as any other sovereign state. The moral persons who live together in a society, subject to international law. To give a state the right to make an immediate figure in this grand society, it is sufficient that it is sovereign and independent, that is that it governs itself by its own authority and laws.

We shall therefore account sovereign states those which have united themselves, to another more powerful, by an unequal alliance, in which the more powerful is given more honor, and to the weaker more assistance. The conditions of those unequal alliances may be varied. But whatever they are, provided the inferior ally reserve to itself the sovereignty, or the right of governing its own body. It ought to be considered as an independent state, that keeps with others under the authority of international law.

A weak state, which in order to provide for its safety, places itself under the protection of a more powerful state, and in return, to preform several offices equivalent to that protection without divesting itself of the right of government and sovereignty. The state does not cease to rank among the sovereigns who acknowledge no other law than international law.

Several sovereigns and independent states may unite themselves together by a treaty without ceasing to be, each individually, an independent state. They will together constitute an international governmental organization. Their joint deliberations will not impair the sovereignty of each member, though they may in certain respects put some restraint on the exercise of it, in virtue of voluntary engagements. A state does not cease to be free and independent, when they are obliged to fulfill engagements which he has voluntarily contracted.

A state that has passed under the dominion of another is no longer a state and can no longer avail itself directly of international law. The generality even of those whom they honored with, the name of allies no longer formed real states within themselves, they were governed by their own laws, but without they were in everything obliged to follow orders, they dared not of themselves either to make war, or contract allegiances and could not treat with states.

International law is the law of sovereigns, free and independent states are moral persons whose rights and obligations we are to establish in this treaty.

Chapter 2: Domestic Duties of the State

If the rights of a state spring from its obligations, it is principally from those that relate to itself, as the former are to be regulated and measured by the latter. As we are then to treat of the obligations and rights of nations, an attention to order requires that we should begin by establishing what each state owes to itself.

The general and fundamental rule of our duties towards ourselves is, that every moral being ought to live in a manner conformable to his nature. A state is a being determined by its essential attributes, that has its own nature, and can act in conformity to it. There are then actions of a state as such, wherein it is concerned in its national character, and which are either suitable or opposite to what constitutes it a state, so that it is not a matter of indifference whether it performs some of those actions and omits others. In this respect, international law prescribes certain duties we shall see, in this book what conduct a state ought to observe, in order that it may not be wanting to itself. But we shall first sketch out a general idea of this subject.

He who no longer exists can have no duties to perform, and a moral being is charged with obligations to himself, only with a view to his perfection and happiness, for to preserve and to perfect his own nature, is the sum of all his duties to himself.

The preservation of a state consists in the duration of the political association by which it is formed. If a period is put to this association, the state no longer subsists, though the individual that composed it, still exist.

The perfection of a state is found in what renders it capable of obtaining the end of a civil society, and a state in a perfect state, when nothing necessary is wanting to arrive at that end. We know that the perfection of a thing consists, generally, in the perfect agreement of all its constituent parts to tend to the same end. A state being a multitude of men united together in civil society if in that multitude all conspire to attain, the state is perfect, and it is more or less so, according as it approaches more or less of states bound by unequal alliance to that perfect agreement. In the same manner its external state will be more or less perfect, according as it concurs with the interior perfection of the state.

The end or object of civil society is to procure for the citizens whatever they stand in need of, for the necessities, the conveniences, the accommodation of life, and, in general, whatever constitutes happiness, with the peaceful possession of property, a method of obtaining justice with security, and, finally a mutual defense against all external violence.

It is now easy to form a just idea of the perfection of a state, everything in it must conspire to promote the ends that have been pointed out.

In the act of association by virtue of which a multitude of men form together a state, each individual has entered into engagements with all to promote the general welfare, and all have entered into engagements with each individual, to facilitate for him the means of supplying his necessities, and to protect and defend himself. It is a manifest that these reciprocal engagements cannot otherwise be fulfilled than by maintaining the political association, and as their preservation depends on its continuance, it then follows that every state is obliged to perform the duty of self-preservation.

This obligation, so natural to each individual of natural creation, is not derived to states immediately from nature, but from the agreement by which civil society is formed, it is therefore not absolute but conditional, that is to say, it supposes a human act, to wit, the social compact. As compacts may be dissolved by common consent of the parties, if the individuals that compose a state should unanimously agree to break the link that binds them, it would be lawful for them to do so, and thus to destroy the state, but they would doubtless incur a degree of guilt, if they took this step without just and weighty reasons, for civil societies are approved by the Law of Nature, which recommends them to mankind, as the true means of supplying all their wants, and of effectually advancing towards their own perfection. Moreover, civil society is so useful, not so necessary to all citizens, that it may well be considered as morally impossible for them to consent unanimously to break it without necessity. But what citizens may or ought to do, what the majority of them may resolve in certain cases of necessity, or of pressing exigency, are questions that will be treated of elsewhere they cannot be solidly determined without some principles which have not yet been established. For the present, it is sufficient to have proved, that in general, as long as the political society subsists, the whole state is obliged to endeavor to maintain it.

If a state is obliged to preserve itself, it is no less obliged carefully to preserve all its members. The state owes this to itself, since the loss even of one of its members weakens it, and or by treaties of protection is injurious to its preservation. It owes this also to the members in particular in consequence of the very act of association, for those who compose a state are united for their defense and common advantage, and none can justly be deprived of that union, and of the advantages he expects to derive from it, while he on his side fulfills the conditions.

The body of a state cannot then abandon a province, a town, or even a single individual who is a part of it, unless compelled to it by necessity or indispensably obliged to it by the strongest reasons founded on public safety.

Since a state is obligated to preserve itself, it has a right to everything necessary for its preservation. The Law of Nature gives us a right to everything, without which we cannot fulfill our obligation, otherwise it would oblige us to do impossibilities, or rather would contradict itself in prescribing us a duty, and at the same time debarring us of the only means of fulfilling it. It will doubtless be here understood, that those means ought not to be unjust in themselves, or such as are absolutely forbidden by the Law of Nature. As it is impossible that it should even permit the use of such means, if on a particular occasion no other present themselves for fulfilling a general obligation, the obligation must, in that particular instance, be looked on as impossible, and consequently void.

By an evident consequence from what has been said, a state ought to carefully avoid, as much as possible, whatever might cause its destruction, or that of the state, which is the same thing.

A state has a right to everything that can help to ward off imminent danger, and to keep at a distance whatever is capable of causing its ruin, and that from the very same reasons that establish its right to the things necessary to its preservation.

The second general duty of a state towards itself is to labor at its own perfection and that of its state. It is this double perfection that renders a state capable of attaining the end of civil society, it would be absurd to unite in society, and yet not endeavor to promote the end of that union.

Here the entire body of the state, and each individual citizen, are bound by a double obligation, the one immediately proceeding from nature, and the other resulting from their reciprocal engagements. Nature lays an obligation upon each man to labor after his own perfection, and in so doing, he labors after that of civil society, which could not fail to be very flourishing, were it composed of none but good citizens. But the individual finding in a well-regulated society the most powerful successors to enable him to fulfill the task which Nature imposes upon him in relation to himself, for becoming better, and consequently happier, he is doubtless obliged to contribute all in his power to render that society more perfect.

All the citizens who form a political society, reciprocally of tributary rates to advance the common welfare, and as far as possible to promote the advantage of each member. Since then the perfection of the society is what enables it to secure equally the happiness of the body and that of the members, the grand object of the engagements and duties of a citizen is to aim at this perfection. This is more particularly the duty of the body collective of all their common deliberations, and in everything they do as a body.

A state therefore ought to prevent, and carefully to avoid, whatever may hinder its perfection and that of the state or retard the progress either of the one or the other.

It may then be concluded, as it has been done before in regard to the preservation of a state has a right to everything necessary for its preservation, that a state has a right to everything without which it cannot attain the perfection of the members and of the state or prevent and repeal whatever is contrary to this double perfection.

It has been observed that a state ought to know itself. Without this knowledge, it cannot make any successful endeavors after its own perfection. It ought to have a just idea of its state, to enable it to take the most proper measures, it ought to know the progress it has already made, and what further advances it has still to make, what advantages it possesses, and what defects it labors under, in order to preserve the former and correct the latter. Without this knowledge, a state will act at random, and often take the most improper measures, it will think it acts with great wisdom in imitating the conduct of states that are reputed wise and skillful, not perceiving that such or such regulation, such or such practice, though salutary to one state, is often pernicious to another. Everything ought to be conducted according to its nature. States cannot be well governed without such regulations as are suitable to their respective characters, and in order to this, their characters ought to be known.

Chapter 3: The Constitution of the State

Every political society must necessarily establish a public authority, to regulate their common affairs, to prescribe to each individual the conduct he ought to observe with a view to the public welfare, and to possess the means of procuring obedience. This authority essentially belongs to the body of society, but it may be exercised in a variety of ways, and every society has the right to choose the mode which suits it best.

The fundamental regulation that determines the manner in which the public authority is to be executed, is what forms the constitution of the state. In this is seen the form in which the state acts in quality of a body politic, how and by whom the people are to be governed, and what the rights and duties of the governors. This constitution is in fact nothing more than the establishment of the order in which a state proposes the labor in common for obtaining those advantages with a view to which the political society was established.

The perfection of a state, and its aptitude to attain the ends of society, must then depend on its constitution, consequently the most important concern of a state that forms a political society, and its first and most essential duty towards itself, is to choose the best constitution possible, and that most suitable to its circumstances. When it makes this choice, it lays the foundation of its own preservation, safety, perfection, and happiness, it cannot take too much care in placing these on a solid basis.

The laws are regulations established by public authority, to be observed in society. All these laws ought to relate to the welfare of the state and of the citizens. The laws made directly with a view of the public welfare are political laws. Those that concern the body itself and the being of the society, the form of government, the manner in which the public authority is to be exerted, those, in a word, which together form the constitution of the state, are the fundamental laws.

The civil laws are those that regulate the rights and conduct of the citizens among themselves.

Every state that would not be wanting to itself, ought to apply its utmost care in establishing these laws, and principally its fundamental laws, in establishing them, with wisdom, in a manner suitable to the genius of the people, and to all the circumstances in which they may be placed, they ought to determine them and make them known with, plainness and precision, to the end that they may possess stability, that they may not be eluded, and that they may create, if possible, no dissension that, on the one hand, he to whom the exercise of the sovereign power is committed, and the citizens, on the other, may equally know their duty, and their rights. It is not here necessary to consider in detail, what that constitution and those laws ought to be, this discussion belongs to public law and politics. Besides, the laws and constitution of different states must necessarily very according to the dispositions of the people, and other circumstances. In International Law we must adhere to generals. We must consider the duty of a state towards itself, principally to determine the conduct that it ought to observe in that great society which nature has established among all states. These duties give it rights, that serve as a rule to establish what it may require from other states, and reciprocally what others may require from it.

The constitution and laws of a state are the basis of the public tranquility, the firmest support of political authority, and a security for the liberty of the citizens. But a constitution is a vain phantom, and the best laws are useless, if they are not observed, the state ought then to watch very attentively, in order to render them equally respected by those who govern, and by the people destined to obey. To attack the constitution of the state, and to violate its laws, is a capital crime against society, and if those guilty of it are invested with authority, they add to this crime a perfidious abuse of the power with which they are entrusted. The state ought to constantly repress them with its utmost vigor and vigilance, as the importance of the case requires. It is very uncommon to see the laws and constitution of a state openly and boldly opposed, it is against silent and gradual attacks that a state ought to be particularly on its guard. Sudden revolutions strike the imaginations of men, they are detailed in history, their secret springs are developed. But we overlook the changes that insensibly happen by a long train of steps that are but slightly marked. It would be rendering states an important service, to shew from history, how many states have thus entirely changed their nature, and lost their original constitution. This would awaken the attention of mankind, impressed thenceforward with this excellent maxim, they would no longer shut their eyes against innovations, which, though inconsiderable in themselves, may serve as steps to mount to higher and more pernicious enterprises.

The consequences of a good or bad constitution being of such importance, and the state being strictly obliged to procure, as far as possible, the best and most convenient one, it has a right to everything necessary to enable it to fulfill this obligation equally of states. It is then manifest that a state has an indisputable right to form, maintain, and perfect its constitution, to regulate at pleasure everything relating to the government, and that no person can have a just right to hinder it. Government is established only for the sake of the state, with a view to its safety and happiness.

If any state is dissatisfied with the public administration, it may apply the necessary remedies, and reform the government. But observe that I say the state, for I am very far from meaning to authorize a few malcontents or incendiaries to give disturbance to their governors by exciting murmurs and seditions. None but the body of a state have a right to check those at the helm when they abuse their power. When the state is silent and obeys, the people are considered as approving the conduct of their superiors, or at least finding it supportable, and it is not the business of a small number of citizens to put the state in danger, under the pretense of reforming it.

In virtue of the same principles, it is certain that if the state is uneasy under its constitution, it has a right to change it.

There can be no difficulty in the case, if the whole state be unanimously inclined to make this change. But it is asked, what is to be done if the people are divided? In the ordinary management of the state, the opinion of the majority must pass without dispute for that of the whole state, otherwise it would be almost impossible for the society ever to take any resolution. It appears then by parity of reasoning, that a state may change the constitution of the state, and whenever there is nothing in this change that can be considered as contrary to the act of civil association, or to the intention of those united under it, the whole is bound to conform to the resolution of the majority. But if the question be, to quit a form of government, to which alone it appeared that the people were willing to submit on their entering into the bounds of society, if the greater part of a free people. Those citizens who are more jealous of that privilege, so invaluable to those who have tasted it, though obliged to suffer the majority to do as they please, are under no obligation at all to submit to the new government, they may quit a society which seems to have dissolved itself in order to unite again under another form, they have a right to self-determination.

Here again a very important question presents itself. If essentially belongs to the society to make laws both in relation to the manner in which it desires to be governed, and to the conduct of the citizens, that is called the legislative power. The state may entrust the exercise of it to the king, or to an assembly, or to that assembly and the king jointly, who have then a right to make new laws and repeal old ones. It is asked whether their power extends to the fundamental laws, whether they may change the constitution of the state. The principles that have been laid down lead us to decide with certainty, that the authority of these legislators does not extend so far, and that they ought to consider the fundamental laws as sacred, if the state has not, in very express terms, given them power to change them. For the constitution of the state ought to possess stability, and since that was first established by the state, which afterwards entrusted certain persons with the legislative power, the fundamental laws are excepted from their commission. It is visible that the society only intended to make provision for having the state constantly furnished with laws suited to particular conjunctures, and for that purpose, give the legislature the power of abrogating the ancient civil and political laws that where not fundamental, and of making new ones, but nothing leads us to think that it meant to submit the constitution itself to their will. In short, it is from the constitution that those legislators derive their power, how then can they change it, without destroying the foundation of their own authority. If a state considers a change, and the whole state was voluntarily silent upon it, it would be considered as an approbation of that act.

But in treating here of the change of the constitution, we treat only of the right, the question of expediency belongs to politics. It shall therefore only be observed in general, that great changes in a state being delicate and dangerous operations, and frequent changes being in their own nature prejudicial, a people ought to be very circumspect in this point, and never be inclined to make innovations without the most pressing reasons, or an absolute necessity. The fickleness is inimical to the happiness of the state, and at length proves fatal to the liberty of which they are so jealous, without knowing how to enjoy it.

It may be concluded from the rights of a state with respect to its constitution and government, that if any disputes arise in a state respecting the fundamental laws, the public administration, or the rights of the different powers of which it is composed, it belongs to the state alone to judge and determine them conformably to its constitution.

All these affairs being solely a state concern, no foreign power has a right to interfere in them, nor ought to intermeddle with them otherwise than by its good offices, unless requested to do it, or induced by particular reasons. If any intrude into the domestic concerns of another state, and attempt to put a constraint on its deliberations, they do it an injury.

Chapter 4: The Sovereign His Rights and Duties

This chapter will not go into a long deduction of the rights of sovereignty, and the functions of a king. Those things are to be found in treaties on the public law. This chapter will show, in consequence of the grand principles of international law, what a sovereign is, and to give a general idea of his rights and obligations.

It has been said that the sovereignty is the public authority which commands in civil society, and orders and directs what each citizen is to perform, to obtain the end of its institution. This authority originally and essentially belonged to the body of the society, to which each member submitted, and ceded his natural rights of conducting himself in everything as he pleased according to the dictates of his own understanding and of doing himself justice. But the body of the society does not always retain in its own hands this sovereign authority, it frequently entrusts it to a government. The government is the sovereign.

It is evident that men form a political society, and submit to laws, solely for their own advantage and safety. The sovereign authority is then established only for the common good of all the citizens, and it would be absurd to think that it could change its nature on passing into the hands of a senate or a monarch. Flattery therefore cannot, without rendering itself equally ridiculous and odious, dent that the sovereign is only established for the safety and advantage of society.

A good king, a wise conductor of society, ought to have his mind impressed with this great truth, that the sovereign power is solely entrusted to him for the safety of the state, and the happiness of all the people, that he is not permitted to consider himself as the principal object in the administration of affairs, to seek his own satisfaction, or his private advantage, but that he ought to direct all his views, all his steps, to the greatest advantage of the state and people who have submitted to him.

A political society is a moral person in as much as it has an understanding and a will of which it makes use for the conduct of its affairs and is capable of obligations and rights. When therefore a people confer the sovereignty on any one person, they invest him with, their understanding and will, and make over to him their obligations and rights, so far as relates to the administration of the state, and to the exercise of the public authority. The sovereign, of the state thus becoming the depository of the obligations and rights relative to government, in him is found the moral person, who, without absolutely ceasing to exist in the state, acts thence forwards only in him and by him. Such is the origin of the representative character attributed to the sovereign. He represents the state in all the affairs in which he may happen to be engaged as a sovereign. It does not debase the dignity of the greatest monarch to attribute to him this representative character, on the contrary, nothing sheds a greater luster on it, since the monarch thus unites in his own person all the majesty that belongs to the entire body of the state.

The sovereign, thus clothed with the public authority, with everything that constitutes the moral personality of the state, of course becomes bound by the obligations of the state, and invested with its rights.

With all that has been said thus far, of the general duties of a state towards itself, particularly regards the sovereign. He is the depository of the empire, and of the power of commanding whatever conduces to the public welfare, he ought, therefore as a tender and wise father, and as a faithful administrator, to watch for the state, and take care to preserve it, and render it more perfect, to better its state, and to secure it, as far as possible, against everything that threatens its safety or its happiness.

Hence all the rights which a state derives from its obligation to preserve and prefect itself, and to improve its state, all these rights, reside in the sovereign, who is therefore indifferently called the conductor of the society, king, superior, etc.

As has been stated, every state ought to know itself. This obligation devolves on the sovereign, since it is he who is to watch over the preservation and perfection of the state. The duty which the law of nature here imposes on the conductors of states is of extreme importance, and of considerable extent. They ought to exactly know the whole state subject to their authority, its qualities, defects, advantages, and situation with regard to the neighboring states, and they ought to acquire a perfect knowledge of the manners and general inclinations of their people, their virtues, vices, talents, etc. All these branches of knowledge are necessary to enable them to govern properly.

The king derives his authority from the state, he possesses just so much of it as they have thought proper to entrust him with. If the state has plainly and simply invested him with the sovereignty without limitation or division, he is supposed to be invested with all the prerogatives, without which the sovereign command or authority could not be exerted in the manner most conductive to the public welfare.

But when the sovereign power is limited and regulated by the fundamental laws of the state, those laws shew the king the extent and bounds of his power, and the manner in which he is to exert it. The king is therefore strictly obliged not only to respect, but also to support them. The constitution and the fundamental laws are the plan on which the state has resolved to labor for the attainment of happiness, the execution is entrusted to the king. Let him religiously follow this plan, let him consider the fundamental laws as inviolable and sacred rules, and remember that the moment he deviates from them, his commands become unjust, and are but a criminal abuse of the power with which he is entrusted. He is, by virtue of that power, the guardian and defender of the laws, and while it is his duty to restrain each daring violator of them, ought he himself to trample them under foot.

If the king be invested with the legislative power, he may, according to his wisdom, and when the public advantage requires it, abolish those laws that are not fundamental, and make new ones.

But while these laws exist, the sovereign ought to maintain and observe them. They are the foundation of the public tranquility, and the firmest support of the sovereign authority. Everything is uncertain, violent, and subject to revolutions, in those unhappy states where arbitrary power has placed its throne. It is therefore the true interest of the king, as well as his duty, to maintain and respect the laws. He ought to submit to them himself.

But it is necessary to explain this submission of the king to the laws. First, he ought, as was just shown, to follow the regulations in all the acts of his administration. In the second place, he is himself, subject in his private affairs, to all the laws that relate to property. When he acts as a sovereign king, and in the name of the state, he is subject only to the fundamental laws, and international law. In the third, place, the king is subject to certain regulations of general polity, considered by the state as inviolable, unless he is excepted to express terms by the law, or tacitly by a necessary consequence of his dignity. The laws that relate to the situation on individuals, and particularly of those that regulate the validity of marriages. These laws are established to ascertain the state of families, now the royal family is that of all others is the most important to be certainly known. But fourth, it shall be observed in general, with respect to this question, that if the king is invested with a full, absolute, and unlimited sovereignty, he is above the laws, which derive from him all their force, and he may dispense with his own observance of them, whenever natural justice and equity will permit him. Fifth, as to the laws relative to morals and good order, the king ought doubtless to respect them, and to support them by his example. But, sixth, he is certainly above all civil laws. The majesty of a sovereign will not admit of his being punished like a private person, and his functions are too be exalted to allow of his being molested under pretense of a fault that does not directly concern the government of the state.

It is not sufficient that the king be above the penal laws, even the interest of states requires that we should go something farther. The sovereign is the soul of the society, if he is not held in veneration by the people and in perfect security, the public peace, and the happiness and safety of the state, are in continual danger. The safety of the state, that then necessarily requires that the person of the king be sacred and inviolable. It is impossible even for the most just and wise monarch, not to make malcontents, and the state ought to continue exposed to the danger of losing so valuable a king by the hand of an assassin. The monstrous and absurd doctrine, that a private person is permitted to kill a bad king. When a king may be, it is an enormous crime against a state to deprive them of a sovereign who they think proper to obey.

But this high attribute of sovereignty is no reason why the state should not curb an insupportable tyrant, pronounce sentence on him, and withdraw itself from his obedience. To this indisputable right a powerful state owes its birth. If the authority of the king is limited and regulated by the fundamental laws, the king, on exceeding the bounds prescribed him, commands without any right, and even without a just title, the state is not obliged to obey him, but may resist his unjust attempts. As soon as a king attacks the constitution of the state, he breaks the contract which bound the people to him, the people become free by the act of the sovereign, and can no longer view him but as an usurper who would load them with oppression. However, as long as a king is in power, he is in command, and the people under him are obliged to submit. It should be remembered the essential end of civil society.

But it is of the utmost importance to observe, that this judgment can only be passed by the state, and that the state itself cannot make any attempt on the person of the sovereign, except in cases of extreme necessity, and when the king, by violating the laws, and threatening the safety of his people, puts himself in a state of war against them. It is the person of the sovereign, not that of an unnatural tyrant and a public enemy, that the interest of the state declares sacred and inviolable. When a king violates the fundamental laws, when he attacks the liberties and privileges of his citizens, or when his government, without being carried to extreme violence, manifestly tends to the ruin of the state, it may resist him, pass sentence on him, and withdraw from his obedience, but though this may be done, still his person shall be spared, and that for the welfare of the state. The very safety of the state requires the person of the sovereign to be held sacred and inviolable, and the whole state ought to render this maxim venerable, by paying respect to it when the care of its own preservation will permit.

Whoever has well weighed the force of the indisputable principles which have been established, will be convinced that when it is necessary to resist a king who has become a tyrant, the right of the people is still the same, weather that king was made absolute by the law, or was not, because that right is derived from what is the object of all political society, the safety of the state, which is the supreme law. It is very difficult to oppose an absolute king, and it cannot be done without raising great disturbances in the state, and the most violent and dangerous commotions, it ought to be attempted only in cases extremity, when the public misery is raised to such a height, that the people may say that it is better to expose themselves to a civil war, then to endure them. But if the king's authority be limited, if it in some respects depends on a senate or a parliament that represents the state, there are means of resisting and curbing him, without exposing the state to violent shocks. When mild and innocent remedies can be applied to the evil, there can be no reason for waiting until it becomes extreme.

But however, limited a king's authority may be, he is commonly very jealous of it, it seldom happens that he patiently suffers resistance, and peaceably submits to the judgment of his people. Can he want support, while he is the distributor of favors? Too many base and ambitious souls, for whom the state of a rich and decorated slave has more charms than that of a modest and virtuous citizen. It is therefore always difficult for a state to resist a king and pronounce sentence on his conduct, without exposing the state to dangerous troubles, and to shocks capable of overturning it. This has occasioned a compromise between the king and the citizens, to submit to the decision of a friendly power all the disputes that might arise between them.

As soon as a state acknowledges a king as its lawful sovereign, all the citizens owe him a faithful obedience. He can neither govern the state, nor perform what the state expects of him, if he is not punctually observed. Subjects then have no right, to examine the wisdom or justice of their sovereign's commands, this examination belongs to the king, his citizens ought to suppose that all his orders are just and salutary, he alone is accountable for the consequences that may result from them.

Nevertheless, this ought not to be entirely a blind obedience. No engagement can oblige or even authorize a man to violate the law of nature.

It is more difficult to determine in what cases a citizen may not only refuse to obey, but even resist a sovereign, and oppose his violence by force. The nature of sovereignty, and the welfare of the state, will not permit citizens to oppose a king whenever his commands appear to them unjust or prejudicial. This would be falling back into the state of nature and rendering government impossible. A citizen ought patiently to suffer from the king, doubtful wrongs, and wrongs that are supportable, the former, because whoever has submitted to the decision of a judge, is no longer capable of deciding his own pretensions, and as to those that are supportable, they ought to be sacrificed to the peace and safety of the state, on account of the great advantages obtained by living in society. It is presumed, as a matter of course, that every citizen has tacitly engaged to observe this moderation, because without it, society could not exist. But when the injuries are manifest and atrocious, when a king, without any apparent reason, attempts to deprive citizens of life, or of those things, the loss of which would render life irksome, who can dispute the citizens right to refuse him. Self-preservation is not only a natural right, but an obligation imposed by nature, and no man can entirely and absolutely renounce it. Though he might give it up, can he be considered as having done it by his political engagements, since he entered into society only to establish his own safety upon a more solid basis. The welfare of society does not require such a sacrifice.

The person of the sovereign is sacred and inviolable, but he who after having lost all the sentiments of a sovereign, divests himself even of the appearances and exterior conduct of a monarch, degrades himself, he no longer retains the sacred character of a sovereign, and cannot retain the prerogatives attached to that exalted rank. However if the king is not a monster, if he is furious only against his citizens in particular, and from the effects of a sudden transport of a violent passion, and is supportable to the rest of the state, the respect citizens ought to pay to the tranquility of the state is such, and the respect due to sovereign majesty so powerful, that citizens are strictly obliged to seek every other means of preservation, rather than to put his person in danger.

A sovereign is undoubtedly allowed to employ ministers to ease him in the painful offices of government, but he ought never surrender his authority to them. When a state chooses a conductor, it is not with a view that should deliver up his charge into other hands. Ministers only ought to be instruments in the hands of the king, he constantly ought to direct them, and continually endeavor to know whether they act according to his intentions. If the irresponsibility of age, or any infirmity, render him incapable of governing, a regent ought to be nominated, according to the laws of the state, but when the sovereign is capable of holding the reins, let him insist on being served, but never suffer himself to be superseded.

Chapter 5: State Successors

It belongs to a state to confer the supreme authority, and to choose the person by whom it is to be governed. If it confers the sovereignty on him for his own person only, reserving to itself the right of choosing a successor after the sovereign's death, the state is elective. As soon as the king is elected according to the laws, he enters into the possession of all the prerogatives which those laws annex to his dignity.

Whenever the chief of an independent state really represents his state, he ought to be considered as a true sovereign, of his representative character, even though his authority should be limited in several respects.

When a state would avoid the troubles which seldom fail to accompany the election of a sovereign, it makes its choice by establishing the right of succession, or by rendering the crown hereditary in a family, according to the order and rules that appear most agreeable to that state. The name of a Hereditary State or Kingdom is given to that where the successor is appointed by the same law that regulates the successions of individuals. The Successive Kingdom is that where a person succeeds according to a particular fundamental law of the state.

The right of succession is not always the primitive establishment of a state, it may have been introduced by the concession of another sovereign, and even by usurpation. But when it is supported by long possession, the people are considered as consenting to it, and this tacit consent renders it lawful, though the source be vicious. It rests then on a foundation that alone is lawful and incapable of being shaken.

The same right may be derived from other sources, as conquest, or the right of a proprietor, who, being master of a state, should invite people, and give them protection, on condition of their acknowledging him and his heirs for their sovereigns. But as it is absurd to suppose that a society of man can place themselves in subjection otherwise than with a view to their own safety and welfare, and still more that they can bind their posterity on any other footing, it ultimately amounts to the same thing, and it must still be said that the succession is established by the express will, or the tacit consent of the state, for the welfare and safety of the state.

It thus remains true, that in all cases the succession is established or received only with a view to the public welfare and the general safety. If it happened then that the order established in this respect became destructive to the state, the state would certainly have a right to change it by a new law. The safety of the people is the supreme law, and this law is agreeable to the strictest justice, the people having united in society only with a view to their safety and greater advantage.

This pretended proprietary right attributed to kings is a chimera, produced by an abuse which its supporters would fain make of the laws respecting private inheritances. The state neither is nor can be a patrimony, since the end of patrimony is the advantage of the possessor, whereas the king is established only for the advantage of the state. The consequence is evident, if a state plainly perceives that the heir of the king would be a pernicious sovereign, the state has a right to exclude him.

The kingdom is the inheritance of the king, in the same manner as his field and his flocks, a maxim injurious to human nature.

A state may, for the same reason, oblige one branch who removes to another state, to renounce all claim to the crown. These renunciations, require or approved by the state, are perfectly valid, since they are equivalent to a law that such persons and their posterity should be excluded from the throne.

It ought to be considered the succession less as a property of the reigning family, than as a law of the state. From this clear and incontestable principle, we easily deduce the whole doctrine of renunciations. Those required or approved by the state are valid and sacred, they are fundamental laws, those not authorized by the state can only be obligatory on the king who made them. They cannot injure his posterity, and he himself may recede from them in case the state stands in need of him and gives him an invitation, for he owes his services to a people who had committed their safety to his care. For the same reason, the king cannot lawfully resign at an unseasonable juncture, to the detriment of the state, and abandon in imminent danger a state that had put itself under his care.

When the state follows the established rule without being exposed to very great and manifest danger, it is certain that every descendant ought to succeed when the order of succession calls him to the throne, however great may appear his incapacity to rule by himself. This is a consequence of the spirit of the law that established the succession, for the people have recourse to it only to prevent the troubles which could otherwise be almost inevitable at every change. Now little advances would have been made towards obtaining this end, if, at the death of a king, the people were allowed to examine the capacity of his heir, before they acknowledged him for their sovereign. It was to avoid these inconveniences that the order of succession was established, and nothing more wise could have been done, since by this means no more is required than his being the king's son and his being actually alive, which can admit of no dispute, but, on the other hand, there is no rule fixed to judge of the capacity or incapacity to reign. Though the succession was not established for the particular advantage of the sovereign and his family, but for that of the state, the heir has nevertheless a right, to which justice requires that regard should be paid. His right is subordinate to that of the state, and to the safety of the state; but it ought to take place when the public welfare does not oppose it.

These reasons have the greater weight, since the law or the state may remedy the incapacity of the king by nominating a successor, as is practiced in cases of minority. This successor is, during the whole time of his administration, invested with the royal authority, but he exercises it in the king's name.

The principles established respecting the successive or hereditary right, manifestly show that a king has no right to divide his state among his children. Every sovereignty, properly so called, is, in its own nature, one and indivisible, since those who have united in society cannot be separated in spite of themselves. Those partitions, so contrary to the nature of sovereignty and the preservation of states, have been much in use, but an end has been put to them, wherever the people, and kings themselves, have had a clear view of their greatest interest, and the foundation of their safety.

But when a king has united several different states under his authority, his empire is then properly an assemblage of several societies subject to the same sovereign, and there exists no natural objection to his dividing them among his children, he may distribute them, if there be neither law nor compact to the contrary, and if each of those states consents to receive the sovereign he appoints for it.

The same principles will also furnish the solution of a celebrated question. When the right of succession becomes uncertain in a successive or hereditary state, and two or three competitors lay claim to the crown, it is asked, "Who shall be the judge of their pretensions?" Some learned men, resting on the opinion that sovereigns are subject to no other judge, have maintained that the competitors for the crown, while their right remains uncertain, ought either to come to an amicable compromise, enter into articles among themselves, choose arbitrators, have recourse even to the drawing of lots, or, finally, determine the dispute by arms; and that the citizens cannot in any manner decide the question.

But, say they, the state has divested itself of all jurisdiction, by giving itself up to a sovereign, it has submitted, it has given to those who are descended from the sovereign's a right which nobody can take from them, it has established them its superiors, and can no longer judge them. Very well! But does it not belong to that same state to acknowledge the person to whom its duty binds it, and prevent its being delivered up to another? And since it has established the law of succession, who is more capable or has a better right to identify the individual whom the fundamental law had in view, and has pointed out as the successor? We may affirm, then, without hesitation, that the decision of this grand controversy belongs to the state, and to the state alone. For even if the competitors have agreed among themselves, or have chosen arbitrators, the state is not obliged to submit to their regulations, unless it has consented to the transaction or compromise, kings not acknowledged, and whose right is uncertain, not being in any manner able to dispose of its obedience. The state acknowledges no superior judge in an affair that relates to its most sacred duties and most precious rights. All the disputes that arise in society are to be judged and decided by the public authority. As soon as the right of succession is found uncertain, the sovereign authority returns for a time to the body of the state, which is to exercise it, either by itself or by its representatives, till the true sovereign be known. "The contest on this right suspending the functions in the person of the sovereign, the authority naturally returns to the subjects, not for them to retain it, but to prove on which of the competitors it lawfully devolves, and then to commit it to his hands.

The state has established the succession, to the state alone belongs the power of acknowledging those who are capable of succeeding.

If education had not the power of familiarizing the human mind to the greatest absurdities, is there any man of sense who would not be struck with astonishment to see so many states suffer the legitimacy and right of their kings to depend on a foreign power?

Finally, there are states whose sovereign may choose his successor, and even transfer the crown to another during his life, these are commonly called patrimonial kingdoms or states, but let us reject so unjust and so improper an epithet, which can only serve to inspire some sovereigns with ideas very opposite to those they ought to entertain. It was shown a state may change the order of succession. But it may happen that a state, either through unbounded confidence in its king, or for some other reason, has entrusted him with the care of appointing his successor, and even consented to receive, if he thinks proper, another sovereign from his hands.

But when a king chooses his successor, or when he cedes the crown to another, properly speaking, he nominates, by virtue of the power with which he is, either expressly or by tacit consent, entrusted, the person who is to govern the state after him. Every true sovereignty is, in its own nature, unalienable. A state becomes incorporated into a society, to labor for the common welfare as it shall think proper, and to live according to its own laws. With this view it establishes a public authority. If it entrusts that authority to a king, even with the power of transferring it to other hands, this can never take place without the express and unanimous consent of the citizens, with the right of really alienating or subjecting the state to another body politic, for the individuals who have formed this society, entered into it in order to live in an independent state, and not under a foreign authority. Let not any other source of this right be alleged in objection to our argument, as conquest. While the victor does not treat his conquest according to those principles, the state of war still in some measure subsists: but the moment he places it in a civil state, his rights are proportioned by the principles of that state.

The state alone has a right to subject itself to a foreign power, the right of really alienating the state can never belong to the sovereign, unless it be expressly given him by the entire body of the people. The right which must be founded on an express consent, on a law of the state, justified by the tacit consent of the people.

If the power of nominating his successor is entrusted to the sovereign, he ought to have no other view in his choice but the advantage and safety of the state. He himself was established only for this end it is solely established for the safety and advantage of society, the liberty of transferring his power to another could then be granted to him only with the same view. It would be absurd to consider it as a prerogative useful to the king, and which he may turn to his own private advantage.

As the safety of the whole state is deeply interested in so important a transaction, the consent and ratification of the people or state is necessary to give it full and entire effect, at least their tacit consent and ratification. As soon as the people submit to the sovereign appointed to rule over them, they tacitly ratify the choice made by the last king; and the new monarch enters into all the rights of his predecessor.

Chapter 6: Principals of A Good Government

It has been shown that a king is entrusted with the obligations of the state, and is invested with its rights, his duty is with the respect to the preservation and perfection of the state, that on his being invested with the sovereign authority, is charged with the duties of the state in relation to government. In treating of the principal objects of a wise administration, let it be shown that the duties of a state towards itself, and those of the sovereign towards his people.

A wise conductor of the state will find in the objects of civil society the general rule and indication of his duties. The society is established with the view of procuring, to those who are its members, the necessaries, conveniences, and even pleasures of life, and, in general, everything necessary to their happiness, of enabling each individual peaceably to enjoy his own property, and to obtain justice with safety and certainty, and, finally, of defending themselves in a body against all external violence what is the end of civil society. The state, or its conductor, should first apply to the business of providing for all the wants of the people, and producing a happy plenty of all the necessaries of life, with its conveniences and innocent and laudable enjoyments. As an easy life without luxury contributes to the happiness of men, it likewise enables them to labor with greater safety and success after their own perfection, which is their grand and principal duty, and one of the ends they ought to have in view when they unite in society.

To succeed in procuring this abundance of everything, it is necessary to take care that there be a sufficient number of able citizens in every useful or necessary profession. An attentive application on the part of government, wise regulations, and assistance properly granted, will produce this effect without using constraint, which is always fatal to industry.

The citizens that are useful ought to be retained in the state, to succeed in retaining them, the public authority has certainly a right to use constraint. Every citizen owes his personal services to his state, and a mechanic, in particular, who has been reared, educated, and instructed in its bosom, cannot lawfully leave it, and carry to a foreign land that industry which he acquired at home, unless his country has no occasion for him, or he cannot there obtain the just fruit of his labor and abilities. Employment must then be procured for him and if, while able to obtain a decent livelihood in his own country, he would without reason abandon it, the state has a right to detain him. But a very moderate use ought to be made of this right, and only in important or necessary cases. Liberty is the soul of abilities and industry, frequently a mechanic or an artist, after having long traveled abroad, is attracted home to his native soil by a natural affection and returns more expert and better qualified to render his country useful services. If certain extraordinary cases be excepted, it is best in this affair to practice the mild methods of protection, encouragement, and to leave the rest to that natural love felt by all men for the places of their nationality.

As to those emissaries who come into a state to entice away useful citizens, the sovereign has a right to punish them severely, and has just cause of complaint against the power by whom they are employed.

In another place, we shall treat more particularly of the general question, whether a citizen be permitted to quit the society of which he is a member. The particular reasons concerning citizens are sufficient here.

The state ought to encourage labor, to animate industry, to excite abilities, to propose honors, rewards, privileges, and so to order matters that everyone may live by his industry.

Chapter 7: The Soil

All the arts, tillage, or agriculture, is doubtless the most useful and necessary, as being the source where the state derives its subsistence. The cultivation of the soil causes it to produce an infinite increase; it forms the surest resource and the most solid fund of riches and commerce, for a state that enjoys a happy climate.

This object then deserves the utmost attention of the government. The sovereign ought to neglect no means of rendering the land under his jurisdiction as well cultivated as possible. He ought not to allow either communities or private persons to acquire large tracts of land and leave them uncultivated. Those rights of common, which deprive the proprietor of the free liberty of disposing of his land, which will not allow him to enclose and cultivate it in the most advantageous manner; those rights, are inimical to the welfare of the state and ought to be suppressed or reduced to just bounds. Notwithstanding the introduction of private property among the citizens, the state has still a right to take the most effectual measures to cause the aggregate soil of the state to produce the greatest and most advantageous revenue possible.

The government ought carefully to avoid everything capable of discouraging the caretaker, or of diverting him from the labors of agriculture. Those taxes excessive and ill proportioned impositions, the burden of which falls almost entirely on the cultivators, and the oppressions they suffer from the officers who levy them, deprive the unhappy peasant of the means of cultivating the earth, and depopulate the country.

Another abuse injurious to agriculture is the contempt cast upon the caretaker. The tradesmen in cities, even the most servile mechanics, the idle citizens, consider him that cultivates the earth with a disdainful eye, they humble and discourage him, they dare to despise a profession that feeds the human race, the natural employment of man.

The cultivation of the soil deserves the attention of the government, not only on account of the invaluable advantages that flow from it, but from its being an obligation imposed by nature on mankind. The whole earth is destined to feed its inhabitants; but this it would be incapable of doing if it were uncultivated. Every state is then obliged by the law of nature to cultivate the land that has fallen to its share; and it has no right to enlarge its boundaries, or have recourse to the assistance of other states, but in proportion as the land in its possession is incapable of furnishing it with necessaries. Those states who inhabit fertile lands, but disdain to cultivate their lands and choose rather to live by plunder, are wanting to themselves, are injurious to all their neighbors, and deserve to be extirpated as savage and pernicious beasts. There are others, who, to avoid labor, choose to live only by hunting, and their flocks. This might, doubtless, be allowed in the first ages of the world, when the earth, without cultivation, produced more than was sufficient to feed its small number of inhabitants. But at present, when the human race is so greatly multiplied, it could not subsist if all states were disposed to live in that manner. Those who still pursue this idle mode of life, usurp more extensive territories than, with a reasonable share of labor, they would have occasion for, and have, therefore, no reason to complain, if other states, more industrious and too closely confined, come to take possession of a part of those lands.

The establishment of public granaries is an excellent regulation for preventing scarcity. But great care should be taken to prevent their being managed with a mercantile spirit, and with views of profit. This would be establishing a monopoly, which would not be the less unlawful for its being carried on by the magistrate. These granaries should be filled in times of the greatest plenty and take off the corn that would lie on the caretaker's hands or be carried in too great quantities to foreign states, they should be opened when corn is dear, and keep it at a reasonable price. If in a time of plenty they prevent that necessary commodity from easily falling to a very low price, this inconvenience is more than compensated by the relief they afford in times of dearth, or rather, it is no inconvenience at all, for when corn is sold extremely cheap, the manufacturer, in order to obtain a preference, is tempted to undersell his neighbors, by offering his goods at a price which he is afterwards obliged to raise, or he accustoms himself to an easy life, which he cannot support in harder times. It would be of advantage to manufactures and to commerce to have the subsistence of workmen regularly kept at a moderate and nearly equal price. In short, public granaries keep in the state quantities of corn that would be sent abroad at too cheap a rate, and must be purchased again, and brought back at a very great expense after a bad harvest, which is a real loss to the state. These establishments, however, do not hinder the corn trade. If the state, one year with another, produces more than is sufficient for the support of its inhabitants, the superfluity will still be sent abroad: but it will be sent at a higher and fairer price.

Chapter 8: Commerce

It is commerce that enables individuals and whole states to procure those commodities which they stand in need of but cannot find at domestic. Commerce is divided into domestic and foreign trade. The former is that carried on in the state between the several inhabitants, the latter is carried on with foreign states.

The domestic trade of a state is of great use, it furnishes all the citizens with the means of procuring whatever they want, as either necessary, useful, or agreeable, it causes a circulation of money, excites industry, animates labor, and, by affording subsistence to a great number of people, contributes to increase the population and power of the state.

The same reasons show the use of foreign trade, which is moreover attended with these two advantages. By trading with foreigners, a state procures such things as neither nature nor art can furnish in the country it occupies. Secondly, if its foreign trade be properly directed, it increases the riches of the state, and may become the source of wealth and plenty.

States are obliged to cultivate the domestic trade, first because it is clearly demonstrated from the law of nature, that mankind ought mutually to assist each other, and, as far as in their power, contribute to the perfection and happiness of their fellow creatures: where arises, after the introduction of private property, the obligation to resign to others, at a fair price, those things which they have occasion for, and which we do not destine for our own use. Secondly, society being established with a view that each may procure whatever things are necessary to his own perfection and happiness, and a domestic trade being the means of obtaining them, the obligations to carry on and improve this trade are derived from the very compact on which the society was formed. Finally, being advantageous to the state, it is a duty the people owe to themselves, to make this commerce flourish.

For the same reason, drawn from the welfare of the state, and also to procure for the citizens everything they want, a state is obliged to promote and carry on a foreign trade.

Let us now see what the laws of nature and the rights of states in respect to the commerce are carry on with each other. Men are obliged mutually to assist each other as much as possible, and to contribute to the perfection and happiness of their fellow-creatures society established by nature between all mankind, where it follows, obligations to cultivate the domestic trade, that after the introduction of private property, it became a duty to sell to each other, at a fair price, what the possessor himself has no occasion for, and what is necessary to others, because since that introduction of private property, no one can, by any other moans, procure the different things that may be necessary or useful to him, and calculated to render life pleasant and agreeable. Now, since right springs from obligation defined by international law, the obligation which was just established gives every man the right of procuring the things he wants, by purchasing them at a reasonable price from those who have themselves no occasion for them.

It is also seen to what laws states are subject, that men could not free themselves from the authority of the laws of nature by uniting in civil society, and that the whole state remains equally subject to those laws in its natural capacity, so that the natural and necessary law of states is no other than the law of nature properly applied to states or sovereign states in what international law originally consist, from all which it follows, that a state has a right to procure, at an equitable price, whatever articles it wants, by purchasing them of other states who have no occasion for them. This is the foundation of the right of commerce between different states, and, in particular, of the right of buying.

Every man and every state being perfectly at liberty to buy a thing that is to be sold, or not to buy it, and to buy it of one rather than of another' the law of nature gives to no person whatsoever any kind of right to sell what belongs to him to another who does not wish to buy it, neither has any state the right of selling its commodities or merchandise to a people who are unwilling to have them.

Every state has consequently a right to prohibit the entrance of foreign merchandises, and the states that are affected by such prohibition have no right to complain of it, as if they had been refused an office of humanity. Their complaints would be ridiculous, since their only ground of complaint would be, that a profit is refused to them by that state who does not choose they should make it at its expense, It is however, true that if a state was very certain that the prohibition of its merchandises was not founded on any reason drawn from the welfare of the state that prohibited them, site would have cause to consider this conduct as a mark of ill will show in this instance, and to complain of it on that fooling. But it would be very difficult for the excluded state to judge with certainty that the state had no solid or apparent reason for making such a prohibition.

By the manner in which has been shown a state's right to buy of another what it wants, it is easy to see that this right is not one of those called perfect, and that are accompanied with a right to use constraint. You have a right to buy of others such things as you want, and of which they themselves have no need, you make application to me: I am not obliged to sell them to you, if I myself have any occasion for them. In virtue of the natural liberty which belongs to all men, it is I who am to judge whether I have occasion for them myself, or can conveniently sell them to you, and you have no right to determine whether I judge well, or ill, because you have no authority over me. If I, improperly, and without any good reason, refuse to sell you at a fair price what you want, I offend against my duty, you may complain of this, but you must submit to it: and you cannot attempt to force me, without violating my natural right, and doing me an injury. The right of buying the things we want is then only an imperfect right, like that of a poor man to receive alms of the rich man, if the latter refuses to bestow it, the poor man may justly complain: but he has no right to take it by force.

Since then a state cannot have a natural right to sell its merchandises to another that is unwilling to purchase them, since it has only an imperfect right to buy what it wants of others, since it belongs only to these last to judge whether it be proper for them to sell or not, and finally, since commerce consists in mutually buying and selling all sorts of commodities, it is evident that it depends on the will of any state to carry on commerce with another, or to let it alone. If the state is willing to allow this to one, it depends on the state to permit it under such conditions as it shall think proper. For in permitting another state to trade with it, it grants that other a right, and everyone is at liberty to affix what conditions he pleases to a right which he grants of his own accord.

Men and sovereign states may, by their promises, enter into a perfect obligation with respect to each other, in things where nature has imposed only an imperfect obligation. A state, not having naturally a perfect right to carry on a commerce with another, may procure it by an agreement or treaty. This right is then acquired only by treaties and relates to that branch of international law termed conventional international law or the law of treaties. The treaty that gives the right of commerce, is the measure and rule of that right.

A simple permission to carry on commerce with a state gives no perfect right to that commerce. For if I merely and simply permit you to do anything, I do not give you any right to do it afterwards in spite of me, you may make use of my condescension as long as it lasts, but nothing prevents me from changing my will. As then every state has a right to choose whether it will or will not trade with another, and on what conditions it is willing to do it, every state is to choose how far it will engage in commerce, if one state has for a time permitted another to come and trade in the state, it is at liberty, whenever it thinks proper, to prohibit that commerce, to restrain it, to subject it to certain regulations, and the people who before carried it on cannot complain of injustice.

States, as well as individuals, are obliged to trade together for the common benefit of the human race, because mankind stands in need of each other's assistance society established by nature between all mankind, and between states, and the foundation of the laws of commerce. Still however, each state remains at liberty to consider, in particular cases, whether it be convenient for them to encourage or permit commerce, and as our duty to ourselves is paramount to our duty to others, if one state finds itself in such circumstances that it thinks foreign commerce dangerous to the state, it may renounce and prohibit it.

If a state has procured the liberty of selling certain merchandises to another, it does not lose its right, though a great number of years are suffered to elapse without its being used, because this right is a simple power, jus merae facultatis, which it is at liberty to use or not, whenever the state pleases.

Certain circumstances, however, may render a different decision necessary, because they imply a change in the nature of the right in question. For instance, if it appears evident, that the state granting this right granted it only with a view of procuring a species of merchandise of which it stands in need, and if the state which obtained the right of selling neglects to furnish those merchandises, and another offers to bring them regularly, on condition of having an exclusive privilege, it appears certain that the privilege may be granted to the latter. Thus, the state that had the right of selling would lose it, because it had not fulfilled the tacit condition.

Commerce is a common benefit to a state, and all its members have an equal right to it. Monopoly, therefore, in general, is contrary to the rights of the citizens. However, this rule has its exceptions, suggested even by the interest of the state: and a wise government may justly establish monopolies. There are commercial enterprises that cannot be carried on without an energy that requires considerable funds, which surpass the ability of individuals. There are others that would soon become ruinous, were they not conducted with great prudence, with one regular spirit, and according to well-supported maxims and rules. These branches of trade cannot be indiscriminately carried on by individuals: companies are therefore formed, under the authority of government, and these companies cannot subsist without an exclusive privilege. It is therefore advantageous to the state to grant them: hence have arisen, in different states, those powerful companies that carry on commerce.

It is also certain beyond all doubt, that, whenever any individual offers, on condition of obtaining an exclusive privilege, to establish a particular branch of commerce or manufacture which the state has not the means of carrying on, the sovereign may grant him such privilege.

But whenever any branch of commerce may be left open to the whole state, without producing any inconvenience or being less advantageous to the state, a restriction of that commerce to a few privileged individuals is a violation of the rights of all the other citizens. Even when such a commerce requires considerable expenses to maintain forts, men of war, etc., this being a state affair, the state may defray those expenses, and, as an encouragement to industry, leave the profits of the trade to the merchants.

The sovereign of a state ought to take particular care to encourage the commerce that is advantageous to his people, and to suppress or lay restraints upon that which is to their disadvantage.

Of all the measures that a wise government may take with this view, only touching on import duties. When the sovereign of a state, without absolutely forcing trade, are nevertheless desirous of diverting it into other channels, he lays such duties on the merchandises they would discourage as will prevent their consumption. Every state has an undoubted right to make what conditions it thinks proper, with respect to receiving foreign merchandises, and being even at liberty to refuse taking them at all.

Chapter 9: Public Roads & Tolls

The utility of highways, bridges, canals, and, all safe and commodious ways of communication, cannot be doubted. They facilitate the trade between one place and another, and render the conveyance of merchandise less expensive, as well as more certain and easier. The merchants are enabled to sell at a better price, and to obtain the preference; an attraction is held out to foreigners, whose merchandises are carried through the country, and diffuse wealth in all the places through which they pass.

One of the principal things that ought to employ the attention of the government with respect to the welfare of the public in general, and of trade in particular, must then relate to the highways, canals, etc., in which nothing ought to be neglected to render them safe and commodious. Numerous patrols everywhere watch over the safety of travelers, magnificent roads, bridges, and canals, facilitate the communication between one area and another

The whole state ought to contribute to such useful undertakings. When therefore the laying out and repairing of highways, bridges, and canals, would be too great a burden on the ordinary revenues of the state, the government may oblige the people to labor at them, or to contribute to the expense.

The construction and preservation of all these works being attended with great expense, the state may very justly oblige all those to contribute to them, who receive advantage from their use, this is the legitimate origin of the right of toll. It is just that a traveler, and especially a merchant, who receives advantage from a bridge, a canal, or a road, in his own passage, and in the more commodious conveyance of his merchandise, should help to defray the expense of these useful establishments, by a moderate contribution: and if the state thinks proper to exempt the citizens from paying it, she is under no obligation to gratify strangers in this particular.

But a law so just in its origin frequently degenerates into great abuses. There are states where no care is taken of the highways, and where nevertheless considerable tolls are exacted. A minister, who happens to possess a strip of land terminating on a river, there establishes a toll, though he is not at a farthing's expense in keeping up the navigation of the river and rendering it convenient. This is a manifest extortion, and an infringement of the natural rights of mankind. For the division of lands, and their becoming private property, could never deprive any man of the rite of passage, when not the least injury is done to the person through whose territory he passes. Every man inherits this right from nature and cannot justly be forced to purchase it.

But international law at present tolerates this abuse, while it is not carried to such an excess as to destroy commerce. People do not, however, submit without difficulty, except in the case of those tolls which are established by ancient usage, and the imposition of new ones is often a source of disputes. This right of tolls is also abused, when the passenger is obliged to contribute too much, and what bears no proportion to the expense of preserving these public passages.

At present, to avoid all difficulty and oppression, states settle these points by treaties.

Chapter 10: Currency

In the first ages, after the introduction of private property, people exchanged their superfluous commodities and effects for those they wanted. Afterwards gold and silver became the common standard of the value of all things, and to prevent the people from being cheated, the mode was introduced of stamping pieces of gold and silver in the name of the state, with the figure of the king, or some other impression, as the seal and pledge of their value. This institution is of great use and infinite convenience: it is easy to see how much it facilitates commerce, states or sovereigns cannot therefore bestow too much attention on an affair of such importance.

The impression on the coin becoming the seal of its standard and weight, a moment's reflection will convince us that the coinage of money ought not to be left indiscriminately free to every individual; for, by that means, frauds would become too common, the currency would soon lose the public confidence; and this would destroy a most useful institution. Hence money is coined by the authority and in the name of the state or king, who are its surety; they ought, therefore, to have a quantity of it coined sufficient to answer the necessities of the state, and to take care that it be good, that is to say, that its intrinsic value bear a just proportion to its extrinsic or monetary value.

It is true, that in a pressing necessity, the state would have a right to order the subjects to receive the currency at a price superior to its real value; but as foreigners will not receive it at that price, the state's gains nothing by this proceeding; it is only a temporary palliative for the evil, without effecting a radical cure. This excess of value, added in an arbitrary manner to the currency, is a real debt which the sovereign contracts with individuals: and, in strict justice, this crisis of affairs being over, that currency ought to be called in at the expense of the state, and paid for in other forms of money, according to the natural standard: otherwise, this kind of burden, laid on in the hour of necessity, would fall solely on those who received this arbitrary money in payment, which would be unjust. Besides, experience has shown that such a resource is destructive to trade, by destroying the confidence both of foreigners and subjects raising in proportion the price of everything and inducing everyone to lock up or send abroad the good old specie; whereby a temporary stop is put to the circulation of money. So that it is the duty of every state and of every sovereign to abstain, as much as possible, from so dangerous an experiment, and rather to have recourse to extraordinary taxes and contributions to support the pressing urgencies of the state.

Since the state is surely for the goodness of the money and its currency, the public authority alone has the right of coining it. Those who counterfeit it, violate the rights of the sovereign, whether they make it of the same standard and value or not. These are called false currencies, and their crime is justly considered as one of the most heinous nature. For if they coin base money, they rob both the public and the king; and if they coin good, they usurp the prerogative of the sovereign. They will never be inclined to coin good money unless there be a profit on the coinage, and in this case, they rob the state of a profit which exclusively belongs to it. In both cases they do an injury to the sovereign; for the public faith being surety for the currency, the sovereign alone has a right to have it coined. For this reason, the right of coining is placed among the prerogatives of majesty.

From the principles just laid down, it is easy to conclude, that if one state counterfeits the currency of another, or if the state allows and protects false currencies who presume to do it, it does that state an injury. But commonly criminals of this class find no protection anywhere, all kings being equally interested in exterminating them.

There is another custom more modern, and of no less use to commerce than the establishment of currency, namely exchange, or the traffic of bankers, by means of which a merchant remits immense sums from one end of the world to the other, at a very trifling expense, and, if he pleases, without risk. For the same reason that sovereigns are obliged to protect commerce, they are obliged to support this custom, by good laws, in which every merchant, whether subject or foreigner, may find security. In general, it is equally the interest and the duty of every state to have wise and equitable commercial laws established in the state.

Chapter 11: Happiness of the State

Experience shows that a people may be unhappy in the midst of all earthly enjoyments, and in the possession of the greatest riches. Whatever may enable mankind to enjoy a true and solid intense happiness, is a second object that deserves the most serious attention of the government. Happiness is the central point where all those duties which individuals and states owe to themselves; and this is the great end of the law of nature. The desire of happiness is the powerful spring that puts man in motion: intense happiness is the end they all have in view, and it ought to be the grand object of the public will to what laws states are subject. It is then the duty of those who form this public will, or of those who represent it, the rulers of the state, to labor for the happiness of the people, to watch continually over it, and to promote it to the utmost of their power.

To succeed in this, it is necessary to instruct the people to seek intense happiness where it is to be found, that is in their own perfection, and to teach them the means of obtaining it. The sovereign cannot, then take too much pains in instructing and enlightening his people, and in forming them to useful knowledge and wise discipline. A just and wise king feels no apprehensions from the light of knowledge: he knows that it is ever advantageous to a good government. If men of learning know that liberty is the natural inheritance of mankind, on the other hand they are more fully sensible than their neighbors, how necessary it is, for their own advantage, that this liberty should be subject to a lawful authority, incapable of being slaves, they are faithful subjects.

In the tender years of infancy and youth, the human mind and heart easily receive the seeds of right and wrong. The education of youth is one of the most important affairs that deserve the attention of the government. The most certain way of forming good subjects is to found good establishments for public education, to provide them with able masters, direct them with prudence, and pursue such mild and suitable measures, that the subjects will not neglect to take advantage of them.

Who can doubt that the sovereign, the whole state, ought to encourage the arts and sciences? To say nothing of the many useful inventions that strike the eye of every beholder, literature and the polite arts enlighten the mind and soften the manners: and if study does not always inspire the love of virtue, it is because it sometimes, and even too often, unhappily meets with an incorrigibly vicious heart. The state and its conductors ought then to protect men of learning and great artists, and to call forth talents by honors and rewards.

What can genius produce, when trammeled by fear? Can the greatest man that ever lived contribute much towards enlightening the minds of his fellow subjects, if he finds himself constantly exposed to the cavils of captious and ignorant bigots, if he is obliged to be continually on his guard, to avoid being accused by innuendo-mongers of indirectly attacking the received opinions? Liberty has its proper bounds, that a wise government ought to have an eye to the press, and not to allow the publication of scandalous productions, which attack morality, or government. But yet, great care should be taken not to extinguish a light that may afford the state the most valuable advantages. Few men know how to keep a just medium; and the office of literary censor ought to be entrusted to none but those who are at once both prudent and enlightened.

To instruct the state is not sufficient, in order to conduct it to happiness, it is still more necessary to inspire the people with the love of virtue, and the abhorrence of vice. Those who are deeply versed in the study of morality are convinced that virtue is the true and only path that leads to happiness; so that its maxims are but the art of living happily, and he must be very ignorant of politics. Who does not perceive how much more capable a virtuous state will be, than any other, of forming a state that shall be at once, happy, tranquil, flourishing, solid, respected by its neighbors, and formidable to its enemies. The interest of the king must then concur with his duty and the dictates of his conscience, in engaging him to watch attentively over an affair of such importance. Let him employ all his authority in order to encourage virtue, and suppress vice, let the public establishments be all directed to this end, let his own conduct, his example, and the distribution of favors, posts, and dignities, all have the same tendency. Let him extend his attention even to the private life of the subjects and banish from the state whatever is only calculated to corrupt the manners of the people. It belongs to politics to teach him in detail the different means of attaining this desirable end, to show him those he should prefer, and those he ought to avoid on account of the dangers that might attend the execution, and the abuses that might be made of them. In general, that vice may be suppressed by chastisements, but that mild and gentle methods alone can elevate men to the dignity of virtue; it may be inspired, but it cannot be commanded.

It is an incontestable truth, that the virtues of the subjects constitute the happiest dispositions that can be desired by a just and wise government. Here is an infallible criterion, by which the state may judge of the intentions of those who govern it. If they endeavor to render the great and the common people virtuous, their views are pure and upright; and you may rest assured that they solely aim at the great end of government, the happiness and glory of the state. But if they corrupt the morals of the people, spread a taste for luxury, effeminacy, a rage for licentious pleasures, if they stimulate the higher orders to a ruinous pomp and extravagance, beware of those corruptors! they only aim at purchasing slaves in order to exercise over them an arbitrary sway.

If a king has the smallest share of moderation, he will never have recourse to these odious methods. Satisfied with his superior station and the power given him by the laws, he proposes to reign with glory and safety, he loves his people, and desires to render them happy. But his ministers are in general impatient of resistance, and cannot brook the slightest opposition, if he surrenders to them his authority, they are haughtier and more intractable than their master, they feel not for his people the same love that he feels. They dread the courage and firmness inspired by virtue and know that the distributor of favors rules as he pleases over men whose hearts are accessible to avarice.

If governors endeavored to fulfill the obligations which the law of nature lays upon them with respect to themselves, and in their character of conductors of the state, they would be incapable of ever giving into the odious abuse. The obligation a state is under to acquire knowledge and virtue, or to perfect its understanding and will, that obligation in relation to the individuals that compose a state, it also belongs in a proper and singular manner to the conductors of the state. A state which acts in common, or in a body, is a moral person, that has an understanding and will of its own, and is not less obliged than any individual to obey the laws of nature, of states bound by unequal alliances, and to improve its faculties, a state ought to prefect itself. That moral person resides in those who are invested with the public authority and represent the entire state. Whether this be the common council of the state, an aristocratic body, or a monarch, this conductor and representative of the state, this sovereign of whatever kind, is therefore indispensably obliged to procure all the knowledge and information necessary to govern well, and to acquire the practice and habit of all the virtues suitable to a sovereign.

As this obligation is imposed with a view to the public welfare, he ought to direct all his knowledge, and all his virtues, to the safety of the state, the end of civil society.

He ought even to direct, as much as possible, all the abilities, the knowledge, and the virtues of the subjects to this great end; so that they may not only be useful to the individuals who possess them, but also to the state. This is one of the great secrets in the art of reigning. The state will be powerful and happy, if the good qualities of the subject, passing beyond the narrow sphere of private virtues, become civic virtues.

The grand secret of giving to the virtues of individuals a turn so advantageous to the state, is to inspire the subjects with an ardent love for their state. It will then naturally follow, that each will endeavor to serve the state, and to apply all his powers and abilities to the advantage and glory of the state. This love of their state is natural to all men. The good and wise Author of nature has taken care to bind them, by a kind of instinct, to the places where they received their first breath, and they love their own state, as a thing with which they are intimately connected. But it often happens that some causes unhappily weaken or destroy this natural impression. The injustice or the severity of the government loo easily effaces it from the hearts of the subjects; can self-love attach an individual to the affairs of a state where everything is done with a view to a single person? On the contrary, that free states are passionately interested in the glory and the happiness of their society.

The love and affection a man feels for the state of which he is a member, is a necessary consequence of the wise and rational love he owes to himself, since his own happiness is connected with that of his society. This sensation ought also to flow from the engagements he has entered into with society. He has promised to procure its safety and advantage as far as in his power.

The state in a body ought doubtless to love itself and desire its own happiness as a state. The sensation is too natural to admit of any failure in this obligation: but this duty relates more particularly to the conductor, the sovereign, who represents the state, and acts in its name. He ought to love it as what is most dear to him, to prefer it to everything, for it is the only lawful object of his care, and of his actions, in everything he does by virtue of the public authority. The monster who does not love his people is no better than an odious usurper, and deserves, no doubt, to be hurled from the throne.

The term, society, seems to be pretty generally known, but as it is taken in different senses, it may not be useless to give it here an exact definition. It commonly signifies the State of which one is a member. A person ought to preserve gratitude and affection for the state to which they are indebted for their education, and of which their parents were members when they gave birth. But as various lawful reasons may oblige one to choose another society, that is to become a member of another society.

If every man is obliged to entertain a sincere love for his country, and to promote its welfare as far as in his power, it is a shameful and detestable crime to injure that very society. He who becomes guilty of it, violates his most sacred engagements, and sinks into base ingratitude: he dishonors himself by the blackest perfidy, since he abuses the confidence of his fellow subjects, and treats as enemies those who had a right to expect his assistance and services. Traitors to their society only among those men who are solely sensible to base interest, who only seek their own immediate advantage, and whose hearts are incapable of every sentiment of affection for others. They are, therefore, justly detested by mankind in general, as the most infamous of all villains.

On the contrary, those generous subjects are loaded with honor and praise, who not content with barely avoiding a failure in duly to their state, make noble efforts in its favor, and are capable of making the greatest sacrifices.

Chapter 12: Morals of a Society

Piety and morals have an essential influence on the happiness of a state. Nothing is so proper as piety to strengthen virtue and give it its due extent. Piety is a disposition of the soul that leads us to direct all our actions, and to endeavor in everything we do. To the practice of this virtue all mankind are indispensably obliged, it is the purest source of their felicity, and those who unite in civil society. The superiors entrusted with the public affairs should constantly endeavor to deserve the approbation of their morals, and whatever they do in the name of the state, ought to be regulated by this grand view. The care of all the people should be constantly one of the principal objects of their vigilance, and from this the state will derive very great advantages. A serious attention to merit, in all our actions, the approbation of an infinitely wise being, cannot fail of producing excellent subjects. Enlightened piety in the people is the firmest support of a lawful authority, and in the sovereign's heart, it is the pledge of the people's safety, and excites their confidence.

When a deluge of bad morals arises, when men are prompted to take methods that are equally false and pernicious. A blind piety only produces superstitious bigots, fanatics, and persecutors, a thousand times more dangerous and destructive to society than libertines are. There have appeared barbarous tyrants who have crushed the people and trampled underfoot the most sacred laws of nature.

So far as it is seated in the heart, it is an affair of conscience, in which everyone ought to be directed by his own understanding, but so far as it is external, and publicly established, it is an affair of state.

Man, doubtless owes the purest love, the most profound respect to their morals; and to keep alive these dispositions, and act in consequence of them. This short explanation is sufficient to prove that man is essentially and necessarily free to make use of his own choice in matters of morals. His belief is not to be commanded. It is impossible that, by his engagements with society, he should have exonerated himself from that duty or deprived himself of the liberty which is absolutely necessary for the performance of it. It must then be concluded, that liberty of conscience is a natural and inviolable right. It is a disgrace to human nature, that a truth of this kind should stand in need of proof.

But we should take care not to extend this liberty beyond its just bounds. In moral affairs a subject has only a right to be free from compulsion but can by no means claim that of openly doing what he pleases, without regard to the consequences it may produce on society. The establishment of morals by law, and its public exercise, are matters of state, and are necessarily under the jurisdiction of the political authority. As this important duty by the state in whatever manner it judges best, to the state it belongs to determine what morals it will follow, and what morals it thinks proper to establish.

If there are no morals established by public authority, the state ought to use the utmost care, in order to know and establish the best. That which shall have the approbation of the majority shall be received, and publicly established by law, by which means it will become the morals of the state. Liberty of conscience is a natural right, and that there must be no constraint in this respect. There remain then but two methods to take, either to permit this party of the subjects to exercise the morals they choose to profess, or to separate them from the society, leaving them their property, and their share of the society that belonged to the state in common, and thus to form two new states instead of one. The latter method appears by no means proper, it would weaken the state, and thus would be inconsistent with that regard which it owes to its own preservation. It is therefore of more advantage to adopt the former method. If there be reason to fear that they will produce divisions among the subjects and disorder in public affairs, there is a third method, a wise medium between the two.

If the number of subjects who would profess different morals from that established by the state be inconsiderable; and if, for good and just reasons, it be thought improper to remain in the state, those subjects have a right to sell their lands, to retire with their families, and take all their property with them. For their engagements to society, and their submission to the public authority, can never oblige them to violate their consciences.

When the choice of morals is already established, the state ought to protect and support those morals, and preserve them as an establishment of the greatest importance, without, however, blindly rejecting the changes that may be proposed to render it purer and more useful. But as all innovations, in this case, are full of danger, and can seldom be produced without disturbances, they ought not to be attempted upon slight grounds, without necessity, or very important reasons. It solely belongs to the society, the state, to determine the necessity or propriety of those changes, and no private individual has a right to tempt them by his own authority. Let him offer his sentiments to the conductors of the state and submit to the orders he receives from them.

But if a set of new morals spreads, and becomes fixed in the minds of the people, as it commonly happens, independently of the public authority, and without any deliberation in common, it will be then necessary to adopt the mode of reasoning.

To give a clear and distinct view of those rights and duties of the king, and to establish them on a solid basis. If there is question of establishing the morals in a state that has not yet done so, the sovereign may favor that which to him appears the true or the best set of morals, and may have it announced to the people, he is even bound to do this, because he is obliged to attend to everything that concerns the happiness of the state.

The king, or the conductor, to whom the state has entrusted the care of the government and the exercise of the sovereign power, is obliged to watch over the preservation of the received morals, established by law, and has a right to restrain those who attempt to destroy or disturb them. But to acquit himself of this duty in a manner equally just and wise, he ought never to lose sight of the character in which he is called to act, and the reason of his being invested with it. Morals are of extreme importance to the peace and welfare of society; and the king is obliged to have an eye to everything in which the state is interested. This is all that calls him to interfere in morals, or to protect and defend them. It is therefore upon this footing that he can interfere: consequently, he ought to exert his authority against those alone whose conduct is prejudicial or dangerous to the state, the punishment of which exclusively belongs to the Sovereign.

The creeds or opinions of individuals, their sentiments with respect to the morals of society, should like piety, be the object of the king's attention, he should neglect no means of enabling his subjects to discover the truth, and of inspiring them with good sentiments. To preserve morals, he ought to maintain them, to take care that they be observed in all its public acts and ceremonies and punish those who dare to attack them openly. But he can require nothing by force except silence and ought never to oblige any person to bear a part in external ceremonies, by constraint, he would only produce disturbances or hypocrisy.

A diversity of opinions and set of morals has often produced disorders and fatal dissensions in a state, for this reason, many will allow but one and the same set of morals. A prudent and equitable sovereign will, in particular conjunctures, see whether it be proper to tolerate or forbid such morals.

The most certain and equitable means of preventing the disorders that may be occasioned by difference in morals, is a universal toleration of all morals which contain no tenets that are dangerous to the state. Do not crush the spirit of persecution, punish severely whoever shall dare to disturb others on account of their creed, and you will see all people living in peace in their common society, and ambitious of producing good subjects.

If in spite of the king's care to preserve the established morals, the entire state, or the greater part of it, should be disgusted with it, and desire to have them changed, the sovereign cannot do violence to his people, nor constrain them in an affair of this nature. The morals of society were established for the safety and advantage of the state, and, besides its proving inefficacious when it ceases to influence the heart, the sovereign has here no other authority than that which results from the trust reposed in him by the people, and they have only committed to him that of protecting whatever morals they think proper to profess.

At the same time, it is very just that the king should have the liberty of continuing in the profession of his own set of morals, without losing his crown. Provided that he protects the morals of the state, this is all that can be required of him. In general, a difference of morals can never make any king forfeit his claims to the sovereignty, unless a fundamental law ordains it otherwise.

The sovereign has a right, and is even under an obligation, to protect and support the morals of the state, and not suffer any person to attempt to corrupt or destroy them. Let the society reconcile those different duties and rights, between which it maybe thought that there is some contradiction, let society if possible, omit no material argument on so important and delicate a subject.

If the sovereign will allow the public exercise the set of morals, let him oblige nobody to do anything contrary to his conscience; let no subject be forced to bear a part in which he disapproves, or to profess a set of morals which he believes to be false, but let the subject on his part rest content with avoiding the guilt of a shameful hypocrisy, let him, according to his own knowledge, in private and in his own house, since it has placed him in such circumstances that he cannot impose his morals without creating disturbances in the state. If any one believes it absolutely necessary, let him quit the society where he is not allowed to practice their morals, let him go and join those who profess the same morals with himself.

The prodigious influence of morals on the peace and welfare of society incontrovertibly proves that the conductor of the state ought to have the inspection of what relates to these morals. It would be certainly very strange that a multitude of men who united themselves in society for their common advantage, that each might, in tranquility, labor to supply his necessities, promote his own perfection and happiness, and live as becoming a rational being, it would be very strange, that such a society should not have a right to follow their own judgment in an affair of the utmost importance, to determine what they think most suitable with regard to morals; and to take care that nothing dangerous or hurtful be mixed with it. Who shall dare to dispute that an independent state, has in this respect as in all others, a right to proceed. When the state has made choice of a particular set of morals, may it confer on its conductor all the power the state possesses of regulating and directing that morals of society, and enforcing their observance.

No person can dispute that the sovereign has a right to take care that nothing contrary to the welfare and safety of the state be introduced into its morals, and consequently, he must have a right to point out what is to be taught, and what is to be suppressed in silence.

The sovereign ought to watch attentively, in order to prevent the established set of morals from being employed to sinister purposes, either by making use of its discipline to gratify hatred, avarice, or other passions, or presenting it in a light that may prove prejudicial to the state. Of wild reveries, seraphic devotions, and sublime speculations, what would be the consequences to society, if it entirely consisted of individuals whose intellects were weak, and whose hearts were easily governed? The consequences would be a renunciation of the world, a general neglect of business and of honest labor. This society would become an easy and certain prey to the first ambitious neighbor.

To the king's inspection of the affairs and concerns of morals we have joined an authority over it. It is absurd, and contrary to the first foundations of society, that any subjects should claim an independence of the sovereign authority, in offices of such importance to the repose, the happiness, and safety of the state. This is establishing two independent powers in the same society, an unfailing source of division, disturbance, and ruin. There is but one supreme power in the state; the functions of the subordinate powers vary according to their different objects, magistrates, and commanders of the troops, are all officers of the public, each in his own department; and all are equally accountable to the sovereign.

Every man in office ought to be vested with an authority commensurate to his functions; otherwise he will be unable to discharge them in a proper manner, only the king should be more particularly watchful that they do not abuse their authority, the affair being altogether the most delicate, and the most fruitful in dangers.

If the sovereign be deprived of this power in matters of society's morals, how shall he preserve the morals pure from the admixture of anything contrary to the welfare of the state? How can he cause them to be constantly taught and practiced in the manner most conducive to the public welfare? How can he prevent the disorders it may occasion, by the manner in which its discipline is exerted? These cares and duties can only belong to the sovereign, and nothing can dispense with his discharging them.

Advancement of this subject, flows from the states of independence and sovereignty, that it will never be disputed by any honest man who endeavors to reason justly. If a state cannot finally determine everything relating to their morals, the state is not free, and the king is but half a sovereign. There is no medium in this case; either each state must, within its own territories, possess supreme power in this respect, as well as in all others.

For an entire body of men, numerous and powerful, to stand beyond the reach of the public authority, and be dependent on a foreign court, is an entire subversion of order in the state, and a manifest diminution of the sovereignty. This is a mortal stab given to society, whose very essence it is, that every subject should be subject to the public authority.

Chapter 13: Justice System

One of the principal duties of a state relates to justice. They ought to employ their utmost attention in causing it to prevail in the state, and to take proper measures for having it dispensed to everyone in the most certain, the speediest, and the least burdensome manner. This obligation flows from the object proposed by uniting in civil society, and from the social compact itself. It has been shown what is the end of civil society, that men have bound themselves by the engagements of society, and consented to divest themselves, in its favor, of a part of their natural liberty, only with a view of peaceably enjoying what belongs to them and obtaining justice with certainly. The state would therefore neglect its duty to itself, and deceive the individuals, if it did not seriously endeavor to make the strictest justice prevail. This attention it owes to its own happiness, repose, and prosperity. Confusion, disorder, and despondency will soon arise in a state, when the subjects are not sure of easily and speedily obtaining justice in all their disputes, without this, the civil virtues will become extinguished, and the society weakened.

There are two methods of making justice flourish, good laws, and the attention of the superiors to see them executed. In treating of the constitution of a state, which ought to establish just and wise laws. If men were always equally just, equitable, and enlightened, the laws of nature would be sufficient for society. But ignorance, the illusions of self-love, and the violence of the passions, too often render these sacred laws ineffectual. In consequence all well governed states have perceived the necessity of enacting positive laws. There is a necessity for general and formal regulations, that each may clearly know his own rights, without being misled by self-deception. Sometimes even it is necessary to deviate from natural equity, in order to prevent abuses and frauds, and to accommodate ourselves to circumstances, and since the sensation of duty has frequently so little influence on the heart of man, a penal sanction becomes necessary, to give the laws their full efficacy. Thus, is the law of nature converted into civil law.

It would be dangerous to commit the interests of the subjects to the mere discretion of those who are to dispense justice. The legislator should assist the understanding of the judges, force their prejudices, and subdue their will, by simple, fixed, and certain rules. These, again are the civil laws.

The laws are useless if they are not observed. The state ought then to take pains to support them, and to cause them to be respected and punctually executed: with this view it cannot adopt measures too just, too extensive, or too effectual; for hence, in a great degree, depend its happiness, glory, and tranquility.

It has been seen that he who is entrusted with the obligations of the state and invested with its rights, that the sovereign, who represents a state and is invested with its authority, is also charged with its duties. An attention to make justice flourish in the state must then be one of the principal functions of the king, and nothing can be worthier of the sovereign majesty. The degree of power entrusted by the state to the head of the state, is then the rule of his duties and his functions in the administration of justice. As the state may either reserve the legislative power to itself or entrust it to a select body. But the conductor of the state must naturally have a considerable share in legislation, and it may even be entirely entrusted to him. In this last case, it is he who must establish salutary laws, dictated by wisdom and equity, but in all cases, he should be the guardian of the law, he should watch over those who are invested with authority, and confine each individual within the bounds of duty.

The executive power naturally belongs to the sovereign, he is supposed to be invested with it, in its fullest extent, when the fundamental laws do not restrict it. When the laws are established, it is the king's province to have them put in execution. To support them with vigor, and to make a just application of them to all cases that present themselves, is rendering justice. This is the duty of the sovereign, who is naturally the judge of his people.

The best and safest method of distributing justice is by establishing judges, distinguished by their integrity and knowledge, to take cognizance of all the disputes that may arise between the subjects. It is impossible for the king to take upon himself this painful task, he cannot spare sufficient time either for the thorough investigation of all causes, or even for the acquisition of the knowledge necessary to decide them. As the sovereign cannot personally discharge all the functions of government, he should with a just discernment, reserve to himself such as he can successfully perform, and are of most importance, entrusting the others to officers and magistrates who shall execute them under his authority. There is no inconvenience in trusting the decision of a lawsuit to a body of prudent, honest, and enlightened men. On the contrary it is the best mode the king can possibly adopt; and he fully acquits himself of the duty he owes to his people in this particular, when he gives them judges adorned with all the qualities suitable to ministers of justice: he has then nothing more to do but to watch over their conduct, in order that they may not neglect their duty.

The establishment of courts of justice is particularly necessary for the decision of all fiscal causes, that is to say, all the disputes that may arise between the subjects on the one hand, and, on the other, the persons who exert the profitable prerogatives of the king. It would be very unbecoming, and highly improper for a king, to take upon him to give judgment in his own cause, he cannot be too much on his guard against the illusions of interest and self-love, and even though he were capable of resisting their influence, still he ought not to expose his character to the rash judgments of the multitude. These important reasons ought even to prevent his submitting the decision of causes in which he is concerned, to the ministers and counselors particularly attached to his person. In all well-regulated states, the ordinary tribunals decide all causes in which the sovereign is a party, with as much freedom as those between private persons.

The end of all trials at law is justly to determine the disputes that arise between the subjects. If therefore, suits are prosecuted before an inferior judge, who examines all the circumstances and proofs relating to them, it is very proper, that for the greater safety, the party condemned should be allowed to appeal to a superior tribunal, where the sentence of the former judge may be examined, and reversed, if it appears to be ill-founded. But it is necessary that this supreme tribunal should have the authority of pronouncing a definitive sentence without appeal, otherwise the whole proceeding will be vain, and the dispute can never be determined.

The custom of having recourse to the king himself, by laying a complaint at the foot of the throne, when the cause has been finally determined by a supreme court, appears to be subject to very great inconveniences. It is easier to deceive the king by specious reasons, than a number of magistrates well skilled in the knowledge of the laws; and experience too plainly shows what powerful resources are derived from favor and intrigue in the courts of kings.

If this practice be authorized by the laws of the state, the king ought always to fear that these complaints are only formed with a view of protracting a suit and procrastinating a just condemnation. A just and wise sovereign will not admit them without great caution, and if he reverses the sentence that is complained of, he ought not to try the cause himself, but submit it to the examination of another tribunal. The ruinous length of these proceedings is to say that it is more convenient and advantageous to the state, to establish a sovereign tribunal, whose definitive decrees should not be subject to a reversal even by the king himself. It is sufficient for the security of justice that the sovereign keeps a watchful eye over the judges and magistrates, in the same manner as he is bound to watch all the other officers in the state, and that he has power to call to an account and to punish such as are guilty of prevarication.

When once this sovereign tribunal is established, the king cannot meddle with its decrees; and in general, he is absolutely obliged to preserve and maintain the forms of justice. Every attempt to violate them is an assumption of arbitrary power, to which it cannot be presumed that any state could ever have intended to subject itself.

When those forms are defective, it is the business of the legislator to reform them. This being done or procured in a manner agreeable to the fundamental laws, will be one of the most salutary benefits the sovereign can bestow upon his people. To preserve the subjects from the danger of ruining themselves in defending their rights, to repress and destroy that monster, chicanery will be an action more glorious in the eyes of the wise man, than all the exploits of a conqueror.

Justice is administered in the name of the sovereign, the king relies on the judgment of the courts, and with good reason, looks upon their decisions as sound law and justice. His part in this branch of the government is then to maintain the authority of the judges, and to cause their sentences to be executed, without which they would be vain and delusive, for justice would not be rendered to the subjects.

There is another kind of justice named attributive or distributive, which in general consists in treating everyone according to his desserts. This virtue ought to regulate the distribution of public employments, honors, and rewards in a state. It is in the first place, a duty the state owes to itself, to encourage good subjects, to excite everyone to virtue by honors and rewards, and to entrust with employments such persons only as are capable of properly discharging them. Also, it is a duty the state owes to individuals, to show itself duly attentive to reward and honor merit. Although a sovereign has the power of distributing his favors and employments to whomsoever he pleases, and nobody has a perfect right to any post or dignity. A man who by intense application has qualified himself to become useful to his state, and he who has rendered some signal service to the state, may justly complain if the king overlooks them, in order to advance useless men without merit. This is treating them with an ingratitude that is wholly unjustifiable and adapted only to extinguish emulation. There is hardly any fault that in the course of time can become more prejudicial to the state, it introduces into it a general relaxation, and its public affairs, being managed by incompetent hands, cannot fail to be attended with ill success. A powerful state may support itself for some time by its own weight, but at length it falls into decay, and this is perhaps one of the principal causes of the revolution's observable in great empires. The sovereign is attentive to the choice of those he employs, while he feels himself obliged to watch over his own safety, and to be on his guard. But when he thinks himself elevated to such a pitch of greatness and power as leaves him nothing to fear, he follows his own caprice, and all public offices are distributed by favor.

The punishment of transgressors belongs to distributive justice, of which it is really a breach, since good order requires that malefactors should be made to suffer the punishments they have deserved. The right of punishing, which in a state of nature belongs to each individual, is founded on the right of personal safety. Every man has a right to preserve himself from injury, and by force to provide for his own security against those who unjustly attack him. For this purpose, he may, when injured, inflict a punishment on the aggressor, as well with the view of putting it out of his power to injure him for the future, or of reforming him, as of restraining, by his example, all those who might be tempted to imitate him. Now, when men unite in society, as the society is thenceforward charged with the duty of providing for the safety of its members, the individuals all resign to it their private right of punishing. To the whole body, therefore it belongs to avenge private injuries, while it protects the subjects at large. As it is a moral person, capable also of being injured, it has a right to provide for its own safety, by punishing those who trespass against it, it has a right to punish public delinquents. Thus, arises the right of the sword, which belongs to a state, or to its conductor. When the society uses it against another state, they make war; when they exert it in punishing an individual, they exercise vindictive justice. Two things are to be considered in this part of government, the laws, and their execution.

The passions might interfere in a business which ought to be regulated only by justice and wisdom. The punishment preordained for a wicked action, lays a more effectual restraint on the wicked than a vague fear, in which they may deceive themselves. The people, who are commonly moved at the sight of a suffering wretch, are better convinced of the justice of his punishment, when it is inflicted by the laws themselves. Every well governed state ought then to have its laws for the punishment of criminals. It belongs to the legislative power, whatever that be, to establish them with justice and wisdom. Each state ought to choose such laws as may best suit its peculiar circumstances.

From the foundation even of the right of punishing, and from the lawful end of inflicting penalties, arises the necessity of keeping them within just bounds. Since they are designed to procure the safety of the state and of the subjects, they ought never to be extended beyond what that safety requires. Whenever a particular crime is not much to be feared in society, as when the opportunities of committing it are very rare, or when the subjects are not inclined to it, too rigorous punishments ought not to be used to suppress it. Attention ought also to be paid to the nature of the crime; and the punishment should be proportioned to the degree of injury done to the public tranquility and the safety of society, and the wickedness it supposes in the criminal.

These maxims are not only dictated by justice and equity, but also as forcibly recommended by prudence and the art of government. Experience shows that the magistrate becomes familiarized to objects which are frequently presented to it. If terrible punishments are multiplied, the people will become less affected by them, and at length contract, a savage and ferocious character, these bloody spectacles will then no longer produce the effect designed, for they will cease to terrify the wicked. It is with these examples as with honors, a king who multiplies titles and distinctions to excess, soon depreciates them, and makes an injudicious use of one of the most powerful and convenient springs of government.

The execution of the laws belongs to the conductor of the state, he is entrusted with the care of it, and is indispensably obliged to discharge it with wisdom. The king then is to see that the criminal laws be put in execution. Besides the reasons already alleged in treating of civil causes, and which are of still greater weight in regard to those of a criminal nature, to appear in the character of a judge pronouncing sentence on a wretched criminal, would ill become the majesty of the sovereign, who ought in everything to appear as the father of his people. It is a very wise maxim that the king ought to reserve to himself all matters of favor and leave it to the magistrates to execute the rigor of justice. But then justice ought to be exercised in his name, and under his authority. A good king will keep a watchful eye over the conduct of the magistrates and he will oblige them to observe scrupulously the established forms. Every sovereign who neglects or violates the forms of justice in the prosecution of criminals, makes large strides towards tyranny, and the liberty of the subjects is at an end when once they cease to be certain that they cannot be condemned, except in pursuance of the laws, according to the established forms, and by their ordinary judges. The custom of committing the trial of the accused party to commissioners chosen at the pleasure of the court, was the tyrannical invention of some ministers who abused the authority of their master. By this irregular and odious procedure, a famous minister always succeeded in destroying his enemies. A good king will never give his consent to such a proceeding, if he has sufficient discernment to foresee the dreadful abuse his ministers may make of it.

The very nature of government requires that the executor of the laws should have the power of dispensing with them when this may be done without injury to any person, and in certain cases where the welfare of the state requires an exception. Hence the right of granting pardons is one of the attributes of sovereignty. But in his whole conduct, in his severity as well as his mercy, the sovereign ought to have no other object in view than the greater advantage of society. A wise king knows how to reconcile justice with clemency, the care of the public safety with that pity which is due to the unfortunate.

The internal police consist in the attention of the king and magistrates to preserve everything in order. Wise regulations ought to prescribe whatever will best contribute to the public safety, utility, and convenience; and those who are invested with authority cannot be too attentive to enforce them. By wise police, the sovereign accustoms the people to order and obedience, and preserves peace, tranquility, and concord among the subjects.

Chapter 14: Fortification Against External Forces

One of the ends of political society is to defend itself with its combined strength against all external insult or violence. If the society is not in a condition to repulse an aggressor, it is very imperfect. It is unequal to the principal object of its destination and cannot long subsist. The state ought to put itself in such a state as to be able to repel and humble an unjust enemy. This is an important duty, which the care of its own perfection, and even of its preservation, imposes both on the state and its conductor.

It is its strength alone that can enable a state to repulse all aggressors, to secure its rights, and render itself everywhere respectable. It is called upon by every possible motive to neglect no circumstance that can tend to place it in this happy situation. The strength of a state consists in three things, the number of subjects, their military virtues, and their riches. One may comprehend fortresses, artillery, arms, ammunition, and, in general, all that immense apparatus at present necessary in war, since they can all be procured with currency.

To increase the number of the subjects as far as it is possible or convenient, is then one of the first objects that claim the attentive care of the state or its conductor, and this will be successfully affected by complying with the obligation to procure the state a plenty of the necessaries of life. By enabling the people to support their families with the fruits of their labor, by giving proper directions that the poorer classes, be not harassed and oppressed by the levying of taxes. By governing with mildness and in a manner which, instead of disgusting and dispersing the present subjects of the state, shall rather attract new ones. That state, so attentive to everything capable of increasing and supporting their power, made wise laws against celibacy, and granted privileges and exemptions to married men, particularly to those who had numerous families. Laws that were equally wise and just, since a subject who rears subjects for the state has a right to expect more favor from it than the man who chooses to live for himself alone.

Everything tending to depopulate a country is a defect in a state not overstocked with inhabitants. It is strange that establishments so directly repugnant to the duties of a man and subjects, as well as to the advantage and safety of society. Should have found such favor, and that king, instead of opposing them, as it was their duty to do, should have protected and enriched them. A system of policy, that dexterously took advantage of superstition to extend its own power, led kings and subjects astray, caused them to mistake their real duties, and blinded sovereigns even with respect to their own interest. Experience seems at length to have opened the eyes of states and their conductors.

A cowardly and undisciplined multitude are incapable of repulsing a warlike enemy. The strength of the state consists less in the number than the military virtues of its subjects. Valor that heroic virtue which makes one undauntedly encounter danger in defense of their state, is the firmest support of the state. It renders it formidable to its enemies, and often even saves it the trouble of defending itself. A state whose reputation in this respect is once well established, will be seldom attacked. If it does not provoke other states by its enterprises. Nature gives the foundation of valor, but various causes may animate it, weaken it, and even destroy it. A state ought then to seek after and cultivate a virtue so useful; and a prudent sovereign will take all possible measures to inspire his subjects with it. His wisdom will point out to him the means.

Valor alone is not always successful in war. Constant success can only be obtained by an assemblage of all the military virtues. History shows the importance of ability in the commanders, of military discipline, frugality, bodily strength, dexterity, and being inured to fatigue and labor. These are so many distinct branches which a state ought carefully to cultivate.

The wealth of a state constitutes a considerable part of its power, especially in modern times, when war requires such immense expenses. It is not simply in the revenues of the sovereign, or the public treasure, that the riches of a state consist: its opulence is also rated from the wealth of individuals. A state is called rich, when it contains a great number of subjects in easy and affluent circumstances. The wealth of private persons really increases the strength of the state, since they are capable of contributing large sums towards supplying the necessities of the state, and that in a case of extremity, the sovereign may even employ all the riches of his subjects in the defense. For the safety of the state, in virtue of the supreme command with which he is invested. The state then, ought to endeavor to acquire those public and private riches that are of such use to it. This is a new reason for encouraging a commerce with other states, which is the source from whence they flow. A new motive for the sovereign to keep a watchful eye over the different branches of foreign trade carried on by his subjects, in order that he may preserve and protect the profitable branches and cut off those that occasion the exportation of money.

It is requisite that the state should possess an income proportionate to its necessary expenditures. That income may be supplied by various means, by lands reserved for that purpose, by contributions, taxes of different kinds.

The law of nature cannot contradict itself, if it forbids an action as unjust or dishonest in its own nature, it can never permit it for any purpose whatever. In those cases where that object, in itself so valuable and so praiseworthy, cannot be attained without employing unlawful means. It ought to be considered as unattainable, and consequently be relinquished.

The power of a state is relative, and ought to be measured by that of its neighbors, or of all the states from whom it has anything to fear. The state is sufficiently powerful when it is capable of causing itself to be respected, and of repelling whoever would attack it. It may be placed in this happy situation, either by keeping up its own strength equal or even superior to that of its neighbors, or by preventing their rising to a predominant and formidable power. A state while it obeys the dictates of prudence and wise policy in this instance, ought never to lose sight of the maxims of justice.

Chapter 15: Glory of the State

The glory of a state is intimately connected with its power, and indeed forms a considerable part of it. It is this advantage that procures it the esteem of other states and renders it respectable to its neighbors. A state whose reputation is well established, especially one whose glory is illustrious, is courted by all sovereigns. They desire its friendship and are afraid of offending it. Its friends, and those who wish to become so, favor its enterprises; and those who envy its prosperity are afraid to show their ill will.

It is then, of great advantage to a state to establish its reputation and glory; hence this becomes one of the most important of the duties it owes to itself. True glory consists in the favorable opinion of men of wisdom and discernment. It is acquired by the virtues or good qualities of the head and the heart, and by great actions, which are the fruits of those virtues. A state may have a two-fold claim to it, first by what it does in its character, by the conduct of those who have the administration of its affairs and are invested with its authority and government. Secondly by the merit of the individuals of whom the state is composed.

A king, a sovereign of whatever kind, being bound to exert every effort for the good of the state, is doubtless obliged to extend its glory as far as in his power. His duty is to labor after the perfection of the state, and of the people who are subject to him. By that means he will make them merit a good reputation and glory. He ought always to have this object in view, in everything he undertakes, and in the use, he makes of his power. Let him in all his actions, display justice, moderation, and he will thus acquire for himself and his people a name respected by the universe, and not less useful than glorious.

The virtues which constitute the glory of kings as well as of private persons, there is a dignity, and decorum that particularly belong to the supreme rank, which a sovereign ought to observe with the greatest care. He cannot neglect them without degrading himself and casting a stain upon the state. Everything that emanates from the throne ought to bear the character of purity, nobleness, and greatness. What an idea does one conceive of a people, when they see their sovereign display, in his public acts, a meanness of sentiment by which a private person would think himself disgraced. All the majesty of the state resides in the person of the king. What then must become of it, if he prostitutes it, or suffers it to be prostituted by those who speak and act in his name? The minister who puts into his master's mouth a language unworthy of him, deserves to be turned out of office with every mark of ignominy.

The reputation of individuals is, by a common and natural mode of speaking and thinking, made to reflect on the whole state. In general, one attribute a virtue or a vice to a people, when that vice or that virtue is frequently observed among them. A state is warlike, when it produces a great number of brave warriors; that it is learned, when there are many learned men among the subjects. It excels in the arts, when it produces many able artists. On the other hand, it is cowardly, lazy, or stupid, when men of those characters are more numerous there than elsewhere. The subjects being obliged to labor with all their might to promote the welfare and advantage of their state not only owe to themselves the care of deserving a good reputation, but they also owe it to the state, whose glory is so liable to be influenced by theirs. On the other hand, the fear of reflecting a disgrace on his state will furnish the good subject, with a new motive for abstaining from every dishonorable action. The king ought not to suffer his subjects to give themselves up to vices capable of bringing infamy on the state, or even of simply tarnishing the brightness of its glory. He has a right to suppress and to punish scandalous enormities, which do a real injury to the state.

Since the glory of a state is a real and substantial advantage, it has a right to defend it, as well as its other advantages. He who attacks its glory does the state an injury, the state has a right to expel him, even by force of arms, a just reparation. One cannot then condemn those measures, sometimes taken by sovereigns to support or avenge the dignity of their crown. They are equally just and necessary. If when they do not proceed from too lofty pretensions, one shall attribute them to a vain pride. People only betray the grossest ignorance of the art of reigning and despise one of the firmest supports of the greatness and safety of a state.

Chapter 16: Voluntary Submission to a Foreign Power

When a state is not capable of preserving itself from insult and oppression, it may procure the protection of a more powerful state. If it obtains this by only engaging to perform certain articles, as to pay a tribute in return for the safety obtained. To furnish its protector with troops, and to embark in all his wars as a joint concern, but still reserving to itself the right of administering its own government at pleasure. It is a simple treaty of protection, that does not all derogate from its sovereignty, and differs not from the ordinary treaties of alliance, otherwise than as it creates a difference in the dignity of the contracting parties.

This matter is sometimes carried still farther. Although a state is under an obligation to preserve with the utmost care the liberty and independence it inherits from nature, it has not sufficient strength of itself, and feels itself unable to resist its enemies, it may lawfully subject itself to a more powerful state, on certain conditions agreed to by both parties. The compact or treaty of submission will thenceforward be the measure and rule of the rights of each. Since the people who enter into subjection resign a right which naturally belongs to them and transfer it to the other state. They are perfectly at liberty to annex what conditions they please to this transfer; and the other party, by accepting their submission on this footing, engages to observe religiously all the clauses of the treaty.

This submission may be varied to infinity, according to the will of the contracting parties. It may either leave the inferior state a part of the sovereignty, restraining it only in certain respects. Or it may totally abolish it, so that the superior state shall become the sovereign of the other. Another option is the lesser state may be incorporated with the greater, in order thenceforward to form with it but one and the same state. Then the subjects of the former will have the same privileges as those with whom they are united.

In the case of a real subjection to a foreign power, the subjects who do not approve this change are not obliged to submit to it. They are allowed to sell their effects and retire elsewhere. For having entered into a society does not oblige them to follow its fate. When it dissolves itself in order to submit to a foreign dominion. People submitted to the society as it was, to live in that society as the member of a sovereign state. Not in another, they are bound to obey it, while it remains a political society. When it divests itself of the quality, in order to receive its laws from another state, it breaks the bond of union between its members, and releases them from their obligations.

When a state has placed itself under the protection of another that is more powerful or has even entered into subjection to it with a view to receiving its protection. If the latter does not effectually protect the other in case of need, it is manifest that by failing in its engagements, it loses all the rights it had acquired by the convention, and that the other, being disengaged from the obligation it had contracted, re-enters into the possession of all its rights. It recovers its independence, or its liberty. It is to be observed that this takes place even in cases where the protector does not fail in his engagements through the want of good faith, but merely through inability. The weaker state having submitted only for the sake of obtaining protection. If the other proves unable to fulfill that essential condition, the compact is dissolved. The weaker resumes its rights, and may if it thinks proper, have recourse to a more effectual protection.

The law is the same with respect to both the contracting parties: if the parties protected do not fulfill their engagements with fidelity, the protector is discharged from his. He may afterwards refuse his protection, and declare the treaty broken, in case the situation of his affairs renders such a step advisable.

In virtue of the same principle which discharges one of the contracting parties, when the other fails in his engagements. The more powerful state should assume a greater authority over the weaker one, than the treaty of protection or submission allows. The latter may consider the treaty as broken and provide for its safety according to its own discretion. If it were otherwise, the inferior state would lose by a convention which it had only formed with a view to its safety. If it were still bound by its engagements when its protector abuses them and openly violates his own, the treaty would, to the weaker party, prove a downright deception.

However, if the state that is protected, or that has placed itself in subjection on certain conditions. Does not resist the encroachments of that power from which it has sought support. If it makes no opposition to them, if it preserves a profound silence, when it might and ought to speak. Its acquiescence becomes in length of time a tacit consent that legitimates the rights of the usurper. There would be no stability in the affairs of men, and especially in those of nations, if long possession, accompanied by the silence of the persons concerned, did not produce a degree of right. It must be observed that silence, in order to show tacit consent, ought to be voluntary. If the inferior state proves that violence and fear prevented its giving testimonies of its opposition, nothing can be concluded from its silence, which therefore gives no right to the usurper.

Chapter 17: A State Within A State

An independent state which, without becoming a member of another state. Has voluntarily rendered itself dependent on, or subject to it, in order to obtain protection. Is released from its engagements as soon as that protection fails. Even though the failure happens through the inability of the protector. One should not conclude that it is precisely the same case with every state, that cannot obtain speedy and effectual protection from its natural sovereign or the state of which it is a member. The two cases are very different. In the former a free state becomes subject to another state. Not to partake of all the other's advantages, and form with it an absolute union of interests. To obtain protection alone by the sacrifice of its liberty, without expecting any other return. When the sole and indispensable condition of its subjection is not complied with, it is free from its engagements; and its duty towards itself obliges it to take fresh methods to provide for its own security. The several members of one individual state, as they all equally participate in the advantages it procures, are bound uniformly to support it. They have entered into mutual engagements to continue united with each other, and to have on all occasions but one common cause. If those who are menaced or attacked might separate themselves from the others, in order to avoid a present danger, every state would soon be dismembered and destroyed. It is essentially necessary for the safety of society, and even for the welfare of all its members, that each part should with all its might, resist a common enemy. Rather than separate from the others, and this is consequently one of the necessary conditions of the political association. The natural subjects of a king are bound to him without any other reserve than the observation of the fundamental laws. It is their duty to remain faithful to him, as it is his. On the other hand, to take care to govern them well, both parties have but one common interest. The people and the king together constitute but one complete whole, one and the same society. It is an essential and necessary condition of the political society, that the subjects remain united to their king as far as in their power.

When a territory is threatened or actually attacked, it must not, separate itself from the state of which it is a member, or abandon its natural king. When the state or the king is unable to give it immediate and effectual assistance, its duty, its political engagements, oblige it to make the greatest efforts, in order to maintain itself in its present state. If it is overcome by force, necessity, that irresistible law, frees it from its former engagements, and gives it a right to treat with the conqueror, in order to obtain the best terms possible. If it must either submit to him or perish, who can doubt but that it may and even ought to prefer the former alternative? A territory submits to the enemy, when it cannot expect safety from a vigorous resistance. It takes an oath of fidelity to him; and its sovereign lays the blame on fortune alone.

The state is obliged to defend and preserve all its members, and the king owes the same assistance to his subjects. If the state or the king refuses or neglects to succor a body of people who are exposed to imminent danger, the latter being abandoned, becomes perfectly free to provide for their own safety, and preservation in whatever manner they find most convenient. Without paying the least regard to those who, by abandoning them, have been the first to fail in their duty.

Chapter 18: Establishment of a State on Land

The earth belongs to mankind in general, to be their common habitation, and to supply them with food. They all possess a natural right to inhabit it and derive from it whatever is necessary for their subsistence, and suitable to their wants. When the human race became extremely multiplied, the earth is no longer capable of furnishing spontaneously. Without culture sufficient support for its inhabitants, neither can it receive proper cultivation from wandering men, continuing to possess it in common. It therefore became necessary that those men should fix themselves somewhere, and appropriate to themselves portions of land. In order that they might, without being disturbed in their labor, or disappointed of the fruits of their industry, apply themselves to render those lands fertile, and thence derive their subsistence. Such must have been the origin of the rights of property and dominion. It was a sufficient ground to justify their establishment. Since their introduction, the right which was common to all mankind is individually restricted to what each lawfully possesses. The land which a state inhabits, whether that state has emigrated towards in a body, or the different families of which it consists were previously scattered over the land. There uniting, formed themselves into a political society, that land is the settlement of the state, and it has a peculiar and exclusive right to it.

The domain virtue of which the state alone may use the land for the supply of its necessities. May dispose of it as it thinks proper and derive from it every advantage it is capable of yielding. The empire, or the right of sovereign command, by which the state directs and regulates at its pleasure everything that passes in the land.

When a state takes possession of a country to which no prior owner can lay claim, it is considered as acquiring the empire or sovereignty of it, at the same time with the domain. Since the state is free and independent, it can have no intention. In settling in the land, to leave to others the right of command. Or any of those rights that constitute sovereignty.

If a number of free families scattered over an independent land, come to unite for the purpose of forming a state, they altogether acquire the sovereignty over the whole land they inhabit. They were previously in possession of the domain. Since they are willing to form together a political society, and establish a public authority, which every member of the society shall be bound to obey, it is evidently their intention to attribute to that public authority the right of command over the whole land.

Mankind has an equal right to things that have not yet fallen into the possession of any one. Those things belong to the person who first takes possession of them. When a state finds land uninhabited, it may lawfully take possession of it. After it has sufficiently made known its will in this respect, it cannot be deprived of it by another state. Thus, navigators going on voyages of discovery, furnished with a commission from their sovereign. Meeting with islands or other lands in a desert state, have taken possession of them in the name of their state. This title is been usually respected, provided it is soon after followed by a real possession.

It is questioned whether a state can, by the bare act of taking possession, appropriate to itself lands which it does not really occupy. Thus, engross a much greater extent of territory than it is able to people or cultivate. It is not difficult to determine that such a pretension would be an absolute infringement of the natural rights of men. Repugnant to the views of nature, which having destined the whole earth to supply the wants of mankind in general. Gives no state a right to appropriate to itself land, except for the purpose of making use of it. Not of hindering others from deriving advantage from it. International law will, not acknowledge the property and sovereignty of a state over any uninhabited lands, except those of which it has really taken actual possession. Which it has formed settlements, or of which it makes actual use.

It is asked whether a state may lawfully take possession of some parts of a vast land mass. Which there are none but erratic states whose scanty population is incapable of occupying the whole. Their unsettled habitation in those immense regions cannot be accounted a true and legal possession. The earth belongs to mankind in general and was designed to furnish them with subsistence. If each state had, from the beginning, resolved to appropriate to itself a vast land mass. The people might live only by hunting, fishing, and wild fruits, the world would not be sufficient to maintain a tenth of its present inhabitants.

When a state takes possession of a distant land, and settles there, that land though separated from the principal establishment, naturally becomes a part of the state, equally with its ancient possessions. Whenever the political laws, or treaties, make no distinction between them, everything said of the territory of a state, must also extend to its territories.

Chapter 19: Native Lands

Subjects are members of the civil society, bound to this society by certain duties, and subject to its authority. They equally participate in its advantages. The natives are those born in the country, of parents who are subjects. As the society cannot exist and perpetuate itself otherwise, then by the children of the subjects, those children naturally follow the condition of their fathers, and succeed to all their rights. The society is to desire this, in consequence of what it owes to its own preservation. It is presumed as matter of course, that each subject, on entering into society, reserves to his children the right of becoming members of it. The state of the fathers is that of the children, and these become true subjects merely by their tacit consent. On their coming to the years of discretion, they may renounce their right, and what they owe to the society in which they were born. In order to be of the state, it is necessary that a person be born of a father and mother who are subjects. If the child is born there of a foreigner, it will be only the place of their birth, and not their state.

The inhabitants as distinguished from subjects, are foreigners, who are permitted to settle and stay in the state. Bound to the society by their residence, they are subject to the laws of the state while they reside in it. They are obliged to defend it, because it grants them protection. Though they do not participate in all the rights of subjects. They enjoy only the advantages which the law gives them. The perpetual inhabitants are those who have received the right of perpetual residence. These are a kind of subjects of an inferior order and are united to the society without participating in all its advantages. Their children follow the condition of their fathers; and, as the state has given to these the right of perpetual residence, their right passes to their posterity.

A state or the sovereign who represents it, may grant to a foreigner the quality of subject, by admitting him into the body of the political society. This is called naturalization. There are some states in which the sovereign cannot grant to a foreigner all the rights of subjects. For example, that of holding public offices, and where he has the power of granting only an imperfect naturalization.

By the law of nature alone, children follow the condition of their fathers, and enter into all their rights. The place of birth produces no change in this particular and cannot of itself furnish any reason for taking from a child what nature has given him. If he has fixed his abode in a foreign state, he has become a member of another society, at least as a perpetual inhabitant; and his children will be members of it also.

Children born at sea, if they are born in those parts of it that are possessed by their state, they are born in the state. If it is on the open sea, there is no reason to make a distinction between them and those who are born in the state. Naturally it is their extraction, not the place of their birth, that gives them rights. If the children are born in a vessel belonging to the state, they may be reputed born in its territories. It is natural to consider the vessels of a state as parts of its territory, especially when they are upon a free sea. Since the state retains its jurisdiction over those vessels. According to the commonly received law, this jurisdiction is preserved over the vessels, even in parts of the sea subject to a foreign state. All the children born in the vessels of a state are considered as born in its territory. Those born in a foreign vessel are reputed born in a foreign state, unless their birth took place in a port belonging to their own state. The port is more particularly a part of the territory, and the mother though at that moment on board a foreign vessel, is not on that account out of the state.

Children born out of the state, in the armies of the state, or in the house of its minister at a foreign court, are reputed born in the state. A subject who is absent with his family, on the service of the state, but still dependent on it, and subject to its jurisdiction, cannot be considered as having quit its territory.

Settlement is a fixed residence in any place, with an intention of always staying there. A man does not, establish his settlement in any place, unless he makes sufficiently known his intention of fixing there, either tacitly or by an express declaration. This declaration is no reason why, if he afterwards changes his mind. He may not transfer his settlement elsewhere. In this sense, a person who stops at a place upon business, even though he stays a long time, has only a simple habitation there, but has no settlement. The envoy of a foreign king has not his settlement at the court where he resides.

The natural or original settlement, is that which one acquires by birth. In the place where their father has his, and one is considered as retaining it. Until one has abandoned it, in order to choose another, the acquired settlement is that where one settles by their own choice.

Stateless people are those who have no settlement. Consequently, those born of stateless parents have no state. A man's state is the place where, at the time of his birth, his parents had their settlement. Or it is the state of which his father was then a member, which comes to the same point. To settle for ever in a state, is to become a member of it. At least as a perpetual inhabitant, if not with all the privileges of a subject.

A man may quit his state or the society of which he is a member. The children are bound by natural ties to the society in which their parents were born. They are under an obligation to show themselves grateful for the protection it has afforded to their fathers. They are in a great measure indebted to it for their birth and education. They ought to love it. To express a just gratitude to it, and requite its services as far as possible, by serving it in turn. They have a right to enter into the society of which their fathers were members. But every man is born free, and the son of a subject. When they come to the years of discretion, they may examine whether it be convenient for him to join the society. If he does not find it advantageous to remain in it, he is at liberty to quit it. On making it a compensation for what it has done in his favor. Preserving as far as his new engagements will allow him, the sentiments of love and gratitude he owes it. A man's obligations to his natural state may change, lessen, or entirely vanish, according as he shall have quit it lawfully. With good reason in order to choose another, or has been banished from it deservedly or unjustly, in due form of law or by violence.

As soon as the son of a subject attains the age of manhood, and acts as a subject, he tacitly assumes that character. His obligations like those of others who expressly and formally enter into engagements with society. Become stronger and more extensive, but the case is very different with respect to him. When a society has not been formed for a determinate time, it is allowable to quit it. When that separation can take place without detriment to the society. A subject may therefore quit the state of which he is a member, provided it be not in such a conjuncture when he cannot abandon it without doing it a visible injury. Every man has a right to quit his country, in order to settle in any other. When by that step he does not endanger the welfare of his state. A good subject will never determine on such a step without necessity, or without very strong reasons. It is taking a dishonorable advantage of one's liberty, to quit their associates upon slight pretenses, after having derived considerable advantages from them, and this is the case of every subject.

Those who have the cowardice to abandon their state in a time of danger, and seek to secure themselves, instead of defending it, they manifestly violate the social compact. By which all the contracting parties engaged to defend themselves in a united body, and they are infamous deserters, whom the state has a right to punish severely.

In a time of peace and tranquility, when the state has no actual need of all its children, the very welfare of the state, and that of the subjects requires that every individual be at liberty to travel on business. Provided that he be always ready to return, whenever the public interest recalls him. It is not presumed that any man has bound himself to the society of which he is a member, by an engagement never to leave the state when the interest of his affairs requires it, and when he can absent himself without injury to his country.

If the body of the society or he who represents it, absolutely fail to discharge their obligations towards a subject, the latter may withdraw himself. If one of the contracting parties does not observe his engagements, the other is no longer bound to fulfill his. As the contract is reciprocal between the society and its members. It is on the same principle. But that society may expel a member who violates its laws.

If the state or the sovereign who represents it, attempt to enact laws relative to matters in which the social compact, cannot oblige every subject to submission, those who are subject to these laws have a right to quit the society, and go settle elsewhere. If the society suffers and is weakened by their departure, the blame must be imputed to the intolerant party. It is they who fail in their observance of the social compact. It is they who violate it and force the others to a separation.

Those who quit their state for any lawful reason, with a design to settle elsewhere, and take their families and property with them, are called emigrants. Their right to emigrate may arise from several sources. It is a natural right, which is certainly reserved to each individual in the very compact itself by which civil society was formed.

This right may be derived from some treaty made with a foreign power. Which a sovereign has promised to leave full liberty to those of his subjects, who for a certain reason desire to transplant themselves into other territories of power. If the sovereign attempts to molest those who have a right to emigrate, he does them an injury. The injured individuals may lawfully implore the protection of the power who is willing to receive them.

Exile is another manner of leaving one's state. An exile is a man driven from the place of his settlement, or constrained to quit it, but without a mark of infamy. Which may be for a limited time, or forever. If an exiled man, had his settlement in his own state, he is exiled from his state. It is proper to observe that common usage applies also the terms exile, to the expulsion of a foreigner who is driven from a state where he had no settlement. To which he is, either for a limited time, or forever prohibited to return.

When the society has excluded one of its members, he is only banished from the lands of that society. It cannot hinder him from living wherever else he pleases, after having driven him out, it can no longer claim any authority over him. The state may take place by particular conventions between two or more states.

Exile is divided into voluntary and involuntary. It is voluntary, when a man quits his settlement to escape some punishment, or to avoid some calamity. It is involuntary when it is the effect of a superior order.

Sometimes a particular place is appointed, where the exiled person is to remain during his exile. Or a certain space is particularized, which he is forbidden to enter. These various circumstances and modifications depend on him who has the power of sending into exile.

A man who is exiled does not forfeit the human character, or consequently his right to dwell somewhere on earth. He derives this right from nature, which has destined the earth for the habitation of mankind. The introduction of property cannot have impaired the right which every man has. To the use of such things as are absolutely necessary. A right which he brings with him into the world at the moment of his birth.

This right is necessary and perfect in the general view of it, one must not forget that it is but imperfect with respect to each state. On the other hand, every state has a right to refuse admitting a foreigner into its territory. He cannot enter it without exposing the state to evident danger or doing it a manifest injury. The state owes to itself, the care of its own safety. Which gives it this right, in virtue of its natural liberty. It belongs to the state to judge, whether their circumstances will or will not justify the admission of that foreigner. He cannot settle by a full right, and as he pleases, in the place he has chosen. But he must ask permission of the sovereign, and, if it is refused, it is his duty to submit.

As property cannot be introduced to the prejudice of the right acquired by every human creature. Not being absolutely deprived of such things as are necessary. No state can without good reason, refuse even a perpetual residence to a man driven from his land. If particular and substantial reasons prevent the state from affording him an asylum, this man has no longer any right to demand it. In such a case the land inhabited by the state cannot, at the same time serve for its own use, and that of this foreigner. Supposing even that things are still in common, nobody can arrogate to himself the use of a thing which actually serves to supply the wants of another. A state whose lands are scarcely sufficient to supply the wants of the subjects, is not obliged to receive into its territories a company of fugitives or exiles. It ought even absolutely to reject them, if they are infected with a contagious disease. It has a right to send them elsewhere, if it has just cause to fear that they will corrupt the manners of the subjects. That they will create occasion any other disorder, contrary to the public safety. It has a right and is even obliged to follow, in this respect, the suggestions of prudence. This prudence should be free from unnecessary suspicion and jealousy. It should not be carried so far as to refuse a retreat to the unfortunate, for slight reasons and on groundless and frivolous fears. The means of tempering it will be, never to lose sight of that charity and commiseration which are due to the unhappy.

If an exiled man has been driven from his state for any crime, it does not belong to the state in which he has taken refuge to punish him for that fault committed in a foreign state. Nature does not give to men, or to states any right to inflict punishment, except for their own defense and safety. It follows that one cannot punish any but those by whom one has been injured.

This very reason shows, that although the justice of each state ought in general to be confined to the punishment of crimes committed in its own territories. People ought to except from this rule those stateless people, who by the nature and habitual frequency of their crimes, violate all public security, and declare themselves the enemies of the human race. Poisoners, assassins, and incendiaries by profession, may be exterminated wherever they are seized. For they attack and injure all states by trampling underfoot the foundations of their common safety. If the sovereign of the state where crimes of that nature have been committed, reclaims the perpetrators of them. In order to bring them to punishment, they ought to be surrendered to him. As being the person who is principally interested in punishing them in an exemplary manner. It is proper to have criminals regularly convicted by a trial in compliance with the law.

Chapter 20: Property

Everything susceptible of property is considered as belonging to the state that possesses the land, and as forming the aggregate mass of its wealth. The state does not possess all those things in the same manner. Those not divided between particular communities, or among the individuals of a state, are called public property. Some are reserved for the necessities of the state, others remain common to all the subjects, who take advantage of them. Each according to his necessities, or according to the laws which regulate their use, these are called common property. There are others that belong to somebody or community, termed joint property. These are with respect to this body in particular, what the public property is with respect to the whole state. As the state may be considered as a great community, which may indifferently give the name of common property to those things that belong to it in common. In such a manner that all the subjects may make use of them, and to those that are possessed in the same manner by a body or community. The same rules hold good with respect to both.

When a state takes possession of land, everything that is not divided among its members remains common to the whole state and is public property. There is a second way whereby a state, may acquire possessions. Which is by the will of whosoever thinks proper to convey to it, under any title whatsoever, the domain or property of what he possesses.

As soon as the state commits the reins of government to the hands of a king, it is considered as committing to him, at the same time, the means of governing. Since the income of the public property, it is destined for the expenses of government. It is naturally at the king's disposal and ought always to be considered in this light. Unless the state has, excepted it in conferring the supreme authority, has provided in some other manner for its disposal, for the necessary expenses of the state, the support of the king's person and household. Whenever the king is purely and simply invested with the sovereign authority, it includes a full discretional power to dispose of the public revenues. The duty of the sovereign, obliges him to apply those revenues only to the necessities of the state. He alone is to determine the proper application of them and is not accountable for them to any person.

The state may invest the king with the sole use of its common possessions, and thus add them to the domain of the state. It may even cede the property to him. But this session of the use of property requires an express act of the proprietor, which is the state. It is difficult to found it on a tacit consent, because fear too often hinders the subjects from protesting against the unjust encroachments of the sovereign.

The people may even allow the sovereign the domain of the things they possess in common, and reserve to themselves the use of them in the whole or in the part. The domain of a river, may be ceded to the king, while the people reserve to themselves the use of it for navigation, fishing, the watering of livestock in that river. The people may cede to the sovereign whatever right they please over the common possessions of the state.

If the income of the public property, is not sufficient for the public wants, the state supplies the deficiency by taxes. These ought to be regulated in such a manner, that all the subjects may pay their share, and the advantages they reap from the society. All members of civil society being equally obliged to contribute, to its advantage and safety. They cannot refuse to furnish the subsidies necessary to its preservation, when they are demanded by lawful authority.

The sovereign possesses the full and absolute authority, it is he alone that imposes taxes, regulates the manner of raising them, and makes use of them as he thinks proper, without giving an account to anybody.

Everything in the political society ought to tend to the good of the community. The state could not subsist, or constantly administer the public affairs in the most advantageous manner. The right which belongs to the society, or to the sovereign, of disposing in case of necessity, and for the public safety, of all the wealth contained in the state, is eminent domain. It is evident that this right is necessary to him who governs, and consequently is a part of the empire, or sovereign power. When the people confer the empire on any one, they at the same time invest him with the eminent domain. Every king who is truly sovereign, is invested with this right when the state has not excepted it.

If the sovereign disposes of the public property in virtue of his eminent domain, the alienation is valid, as having been made with sufficient powers.

Besides the eminent domain, the sovereignty gives a right of another nature over all public, common, and private property. That is the empire, or the right of command in all places of the land belonging to the state. The supreme power extends to everything that passes in the state, wherever it is transacted. The sovereign commands in all public places, on rivers, on highways and deserts. Everything that happens there is subject to his authority.

In virtue of the same authority, the sovereign may make laws to regulate the manner in which common property is to be used, as well the property of the state at large. He cannot take away their right from those who have a share in that property. But the care he ought to take of the public repose, and of the common advantage of the subjects, gives him doubtless a right to establish laws tending to this end. Consequently, to regulate the manner in which things possessed in common are to be enjoyed. This affair might give room for abuses, and excite disturbances, which it is important to the state to prevent. Against which the king is obliged to take just measures. The sovereign may establish wise laws with respect to hunting and fishing, forbid them in the seasons of propagation, prohibit the use of certain nets, and of every destructive method. It is only in the character of the common guardian of his people, that the sovereign has a right to make those laws. He ought never to lose sight of the ends which he is called upon to accomplish by enacting them. If upon those subjects, he makes any regulations with any other view than that of the public welfare, he abuses his power.

A proprietor has a right to alienate and mortgage its property, but the present members ought never to lose sight of the destination of that joint property. Nor dispose of it otherwise than for the advantage of the body, or in cases of necessity. If they alienate it with any other view, they abuse their power, and transgress against the duty they own to their own corporation and their posterity. The king, in quality of common father, has a right to oppose the measure. The interest of the state requires that the property of corporations be not squandered away. Which gives the king entrusted with the care of watching over the public safety, a new right to prevent the alienation of such property. It is very proper to ordain in a state, that the alienation of the property of corporations should be invalid, without the consent of the superior powers. Indeed, the civil law, in this respect gives to corporations the rights of minors. This is strictly no more than a civil law, and the opinion of those who make the law of nature alone a sufficient authority to take from a corporation the power of alienating their property without the consent of the sovereign.

All the members of the state have an equal right to the use of its common property. Respecting the manner of enjoying it, the state may make such regulations as they think proper, provided that those regulations be not inconsistent with that equality which ought to be preserved in a communion of property.

All the members of a body having an equal right to its common property, each individual ought so to manage in taking advantage of it. As not to injure the common use. According to this rule, an individual is not permitted to construct upon any river that is public property, any work capable of rendering it less convenient for the use of everyone else. Such as erecting mills, making a trench to turn the water upon his own lands or in any way restrict its natural state. If he attempts it, he arrogates to himself a private right, derogatory to the common right of the public.

The right of anticipation shall be faithfully observed in the use of common things, which cannot be used by several persons at the same time. This name is given to the right which the first comer acquires to the use of things of this nature. The same rule ought to be observed in regard to those common things which are consumed in using them. They belong to the person who first takes possession of them with the intention of applying them to his own use. Anyone who comes after, has no right to take them from him.

The expenses necessary for the preservation or reparation of the things that belong to the public, shall be equally borne by all who have a share in them. Whether the necessary sums be drawn from the common coffer, or that each individual contributes his quota. The state may establish extraordinary taxes, imposts, or annual contributions, to defray these expenses. Provided there is no oppressive exaction in the case, and that the money so levied be faithfully applied to the use for which it was raised.

The sovereign ought to provide for the preservation of the public property. It is the interest of the state at large that a corporation should not fall into indigence by the ill conduct of its members for the time being. As every obligation generates the correspondent right which is necessary to discharge it. The sovereign has a right to oblige the corporation to conform to their duty. If he perceives that they suffer their necessary buildings to fall to ruin, or that they destroy their forests, he has a right to prescribe what they ought to do, and to put his orders in force.

Every proprietor has a right to make what use he pleases of his own substance, and to dispose of it as he pleases. When the rights of a third person are not involved in the business, the sovereign as the father of his people, may and ought to set bounds to a prodigal, and to prevent his running to ruin, especially if this prodigal be the father of a family. He must take care not to extend this right of inspection so far as to lay a restraint on his subjects in the administration of their affairs. Which would be no less injurious to the true welfare of the state, than to the just liberty of the subjects. The particulars of this subject belong to public law and politics.

Individuals are not so perfectly free in the economy or government of their affairs as not to be subject to the laws and regulations of police made by the sovereign. When a reason of such importance requires it, the sovereign may oblige an individual to sell all the provisions in his possession. Above what are necessary for the subsistence of his family and may fix the price he shall receive for them. The public authority may and ought to hinder monopolies, and suppress all practices tending to raise the price of provisions.

Every man may naturally choose the person to whom he would leave his property after his death. As long as his right is not limited by some indispensable obligation. For example, that of providing for the subsistence of his children. The children also have naturally a right to inherit their father's property in equal proportions. But this is no reason why particular laws may not be established in a state, with regard to testaments and inheritances. A respect being paid to the essential laws of nature.

Chapter 21: Public Property

The state being the sole mistress of the property in its possession, may dispose of it as it thinks proper, and may lawfully alienate or mortgage it. This right is a necessary consequence of the full and absolute domain. The exercise of it is restrained by the law of nature, only with respect to proprietors who have not the use of reason necessary for the management of their affairs. Which is not the case with a state. Those who think otherwise, cannot allege any solid reason for their opinion. It would follow from their principles that no safe contract can be entered into with any state. A conclusion which attacks the foundation of all public treaties.

The state ought carefully to preserve its public property, make a proper use of it, not to dispose of it without good reasons, nor to alienate or mortgage it but for a manifest public advantage, or in case of a pressing necessity. This is an evident consequence of the duties a state owes to itself. The public property is extremely useful and even necessary to the state; and it cannot squander it improperly without injuring itself. Shamefully neglecting the duty of self-preservation, public property or the domain of the state. Alienating its revenues is cutting the strength of the government. As to the property common to all the subjects, the state does an injury to those who derive advantage from it. If it alienates it without necessity, or without cogent reasons, the state has a right to do this as proprietor of these possessions. The state shall not to dispose of them except in a manner that is consistent with the duties which the body owes its members.

The same duties lie on the king, the director of the state: he ought to watch over the preservation and prudent management of the public property. To prevent all waste of it, and not suffer it to be applied to improper uses.

The king being naturally no more than the administrator, and not the proprietor of the state, his authority as sovereign or head of the state, does not of itself give him a right to alienate or mortgage the public property. The general rule is that the sovereign cannot dispose of the public property. If the superior exceeds his powers with respect to this property, the alienation he makes of it will be invalid. It may at any time be revoked by his successor, or by the state.

The state having the free disposal of all the property belonging to it, may convey its right to the sovereign, and consequently confer upon him that of alienating and mortgaging the public property. This right is not necessary to the conductor of the state, to enable him to render the people happy by his government. It is not to be presumed that the state has given it to him.

It is necessary that states should be able to treat, and contract validly with each other. They would otherwise find it impossible to bring their affairs to an issue, or to obtain the blessings of peace with any degree of certainty. When a state has ceded any part of its property to another, the cession ought to be deemed valid and irrevocable. In fact, it is, in virtue of the notion of property, this principle cannot be shaken by any law by which a state might pretend to deprive themselves of the power of alienating what belongs to them. This would be depriving themselves of all power to form contracts with other states or attempting to deceive them. A state with such a law ought never to treat concerning its property. If it is obliged to it by necessity or determined to do it for its own advantage. The moment it breaches a treaty on the subject, it renounces its law. It is seldom disputed that an entire state may alienate what belongs to itself.

When the state has conferred the full sovereignty on its conductor, it has entrusted to him the care, without reserve, given him the right, of treating and contracting with other states. It is having invested him with all the powers necessary to make a valid contract. What the king does is considered as the act of the state itself. Though he is not the owner of the public property, his alienation of it is valid, as being duly authorized.

When the laws forbid all dismemberment by the sovereign, he cannot do it without the concurrence of the state or its representatives. If the laws are silent, and if the king has received a full and absolute authority, he is then the depository of the rights of the state. The organ by which it declares its will. The state ought never to abandon its members but in a case of necessity, or with a view to the public safety, and to preserve itself from total ruin. The king shall not to give them up except for the same reasons. Since he has received an absolute authority, it belongs to him to judge of the necessity of the case, and of what the safety of the state requires.

Chapter 22: Waterways

When a state takes possession of land, with a view to settle there, it takes possession of everything included in it, lakes, rivers and everything else on the land. But it may happen that the land is bounded and separated from another by a body of water. In which case it is asked, to whom this water belongs to. It ought to belong to the state who first took possession of it.

When a state takes possession of land bounded by a river, it is considered as appropriating to itself the river also. The utility of a river is too great to admit a supposition that the state did not intend to reserve it to itself. The state that first established its dominion on one of the banks of the river is considered as being the first possessor of all that part of the river which bounds its territory. When there is a question of a very broad river, this presumption admits not of a doubt, as relates to a part of the river's width. The strength of the presumption increases or diminishes in an inverse ratio with the width of a river. The narrower the river is, the more the safety and convenience of its use require that it should be subject entirely to the empire and property of that state.

If the state has made any use of the river, as for navigating or fishing, it is presumed with the greatest certainty that it has resolved to appropriate the river to its own use.

If two states inhabiting the opposite banks of the river, neither party can prove that they themselves, or those whose rights they inherit, were the first settlers in those tracts. It is to be supposed that both states came there at the same time. Neither of them can give any reason for claiming the preference; and in this case the dominion of each will extend to the middle of the river.

An undisputed possession establishes the right of state. Otherwise there could be no peace, no stability between them. Notorious facts must be admitted proving the possession. When from time immemorial a state has, without contradiction, exercised the sovereignty upon a river which forms its boundary. Nobody can dispute with that state the supreme dominion over the river in question.

If treaties determine anything on this question, they must be observed. To decide it by accurate and express stipulations, is the safest mode. Such is in fact, the method taken by most powers at present.

If a river leaves its bed, whether it be dried up or takes its course elsewhere, the bed belongs to the owner of the river. The bed is a part of the river, and he who had appropriated to himself the whole, had necessarily appropriated to himself all its parts.

If a territory which terminates on a river has no other boundary than that river, it is one of those territories that have natural or indeterminate bounds. It enjoys the right of alluvion. Every gradual increase of soil, every addition which the current of the river may make to its bank on that side, is an addition to that territory. It stands in the same predicament with it and belongs to the same owner.

In case of doubt, every territory terminating on a river is presumed to have no other boundary than the river itself. Nothing is more natural than to take a river for a boundary, when a settlement is made. Wherever there is a doubt, that is always to be presumed which is most natural and most probable.

As soon as it is determined that a river constitutes the boundary line between two territories. Whether it remains common to the inhabitants on each side of its banks, or whether each shares half of it. Whether it belongs entirely to one of them, their rights with respect to the river are in no ways changed by the alluvion. If it happens that, by a natural effect of the current, one of the two territories receive an increase, while the river gradually encroaches on the opposite bank. The river still remains the natural boundary of the two territories. Notwithstanding the progressive changes in its course, each retains over it the same rights which it possessed before. If it is divided in the middle between the owners of the opposite banks, that middle though it changes its place, will continue to be the line of separation between the two neighbors. The one loses, it is true, while the other gains. Nature alone produces this change. It destroys the land of the one, while it forms new land for the other. The case cannot be otherwise determined, since they have taken the river alone for their limits.

Instead of a gradual and progressive change of its bed, the river, by an accident merely natural, turns entirely out of its course. It runs into one of the two neighboring states, the bed which it has abandoned becomes their boundary. It remains the property of the former owner of the river. The river itself is annihilated in all that part, while it is reproduced in its new bed.

This is very different from a river which changes its course without going out of the same state. In its new course it continues to belong to its former owner. Whether that owner be the state, or any individual to whom the state has given it. Because rivers belong to the public in whatever part of the land in which they flow. Of the bed which it has abandoned, a moiety accrues to the contiguous lands on each side. If there are lands that have natural boundaries, with the right of alluvion, that bed is no longer the property of the public, because of the right of alluvion vested in the owners of its banks. Because the public held possession of the bed only on account of it containing a river. If the adjacent lands do not have natural boundaries, the public still retains the property of the bed. The new soil over which the river takes its course is lost to the proprietor, because all the rivers in the country belong to the public.

It is not allowable to raise any works on the bank of a river, which tend to turn its course, and to cast it upon the opposite bank. It would be promoting one's own advantage at their neighbor's expense. Each can only secure himself and hinder the current from undermining and carrying away his land.

If a river belongs to one state, and another has an incontestable right to navigate it, the former cannot erect upon it a dam or a mill which might render it unfit for navigation. The right which the owners of the river possess in this case is only that of a limited property. In the exercise of it, they are bound to respect the rights of others.

When two different rights to the same thing happen to clash with each other, it is not always easy to determine which ought to yield to the other. It cannot be satisfactorily decided, without attentively considering the nature of the rights and their origin. As the proprietor, one has an essential right over the river itself.

The case is different with respect to the right of navigation. This right necessarily supposes that the river shall remain free and navigable, and therefore excludes every work that will entirely interrupt its navigation.

The antiquity and origin of the rights serve, no less than their nature, to determine the question. The more ancient right, is to be exerted in its full extent. The other only so far as it may be extended without prejudice to the former. It can only be established on this fooling, unless the possessor of the first right has expressly consented to its being limited.

Rights ceded by the proprietor of anything are considered as ceded without prejudice to the other rights that belong to him. Only so far as they are consistent with these latter, unless an express declaration, or the very nature of the right, determine it otherwise. If one has ceded to another the right of fishing in their river. It is manifest that they have ceded it without prejudice to their other rights. They remain free to build on that river such works as they think proper. Even though they should injure the fishery, provided they do not altogether destroy it. A work of this latter kind, such as a dam that would hinder the fish from ascending it could not be built but in case of necessity, and on making, according to circumstances, an adequate compensation to the person who has a right to fish there.

What is true of rivers and streams, may be easily applied to lakes. Every lake, entirely included in the land, belongs to the state that is the proprietor of that land. In taking possession of a territory, a state is considered as having appropriated to itself everything included in it.

As it seldom happens that the property of a lake of any considerable extent falls to the share of individuals, it remains common to the state. If this lake is situated between two states, it is presumed to be divided between them at the middle, while there is no title, no constant and manifest custom, to determine otherwise.

When a lake which bounds a state belongs entirely to it, every increase in the extent of that lake falls under the same predicament as the lake itself. It is necessary that the increase should be insensible, as that of land in alluvion, and moreover that it be real, constant, and complete. If the lake, overflowing its banks, inundates a large tract of land, this new portion of the lake, this tract covered with water, still belongs to its former owner. What principles can one found the acquisition of it in behalf of the owner of the lake? The space is very easily identified, though it has changed its nature. It is too considerable to admit a presumption that the owner had no intention to preserve it to himself, notwithstanding the changes that might happen to it.

If the lake insensibly undermines a part of the opposite territory, destroys it, and renders it impossible to be known. By fixing itself there, and adding it to its bed, that part of the territory is lost to its former owner; it no longer exists. The whole of the lake increased still belongs to the same state as before.

Some of the lands bordering on the lake are only overflowed at high water, this transient accident cannot produce any change in their dependence. The reason why the soil which the lake invades by little belongs to the owner of the lake. It is lost to its former proprietor, because the proprietor has no other boundary than the lake. Not having any other marks than its banks, to ascertain how far his possessions extend. If the water advances insensibly, he loses. If it retires in like manner, he gains. Such is the intention of the states who have respectively appropriated to themselves the lake, and the adjacent lands. It can be supposed that they had any other intention. A territory overflowed for a time is not confounded with the rest of the lake. It can still be recognized; and the owner may still retain his right of property in it.

If the waters of the lake, penetrating by an opening into the neighboring lands. There form a bay, or new lake, joined to the first by a canal. The new body of water and the canal belong to the owner of the land in which they are formed. The boundaries are easily ascertained. One is not to presume an intention of relinquishing so considerable a tract of land in case of it happening to be invaded by the waters of an adjoining lake.

If the lake insensibly forms an accession of land on its banks, either by retiring or in any other manner, this increase of land belongs to the land which it joins, when that land has no other boundary than the lake. It is the same thing as alluvion on the banks of the river.

If the lake happened to be suddenly dried up, either totally or in a great part of it, the bed would remain in the possession of the sovereign of the lake. The nature of the soil sufficiently marking out the limits.

The jurisdiction over lakes and rivers is subject to the same rules as the property of them. Each state naturally possesses it over the whole or the part of which it possesses the domain. The state or its sovereign, commands in all places in its possession.

Chapter 23: The Sea

To complete the exposition of the principles of international law with respect to the things a state may possess, it remains to treat the open sea. The use of the open sea consists in navigation, and in fishing. Along its coasts it is moreover of use for the procuring of several things found near the shore, such as shell-fish, amber, pearls and natural resources.

The open sea is not of such a nature as to admit the holding possession of it. But a state powerful at sea may forbid others to fish in it and to navigate it. Declaring that it appropriates to itself the dominion over it. That they will destroy the vessels that shall dare to appear in it without the state's permission.

It is manifest that the use of the open sea, which consists in navigation and fishing, is innocent and inexhaustible. He who navigates or fishes in the open sea does no injury to anyone. The sea in these two respects, is sufficient for all mankind. Nature does not give to man a right of appropriating to himself things that may be innocently used. That are inexhaustible, and sufficient for all. Since those things, while common to all, are sufficient to supply the wants of each. Whoever should to the exclusion of all other participants, attempt to render himself sole proprietor of them, would unreasonably wrest the bounteous gifts of nature from the parties excluded. The earth no longer furnishing, without culture, the things necessary or useful to the human race. It becomes necessary to introduce the right of property. In order that each might apply himself with more success to the cultivation of what had fallen to his share. To multiply by his labor, the necessaries and conveniences of life. The law of nature approves the rights of dominion and property. Which put an end to the primitive manner of living in common. This reason cannot apply to things which are in themselves inexhaustible. Consequently, it cannot furnish any just grounds for seizing the exclusive possession of them. If the free and common use of a thing of this nature was prejudicial or dangerous to a state, the care of their own safety would authorize them to reduce that thing under their own dominion. In order to restrict the use of it by such precautions as prudence might dictate to them. This is not the case with the open sea, on which people may sail and fish without the least prejudice to any person whatsoever, and without putting any one in danger. No state has a right to take possession of the open sea, or claim the sole use of it, to the exclusion of other states.

The right of navigating and fishing in the open sea being then a right common to all men. Any state that attempts to exclude another from that advantage does it an injury and furnishes it with sufficient grounds for commencing hostilities. Since nature authorizes a state to repel an injury. That is to make use of force against whoever would deprive them of their rights.

A state without a legitimate claim, would arrogate to itself an exclusive right to the sea. Support its pretensions by force, does an injury to all states. It infringes their common right, and they are justifiable in forming a general combination against it. States have the greatest interest in causing international law, to be universally respected. If anyone openly tramples it underfoot, they all may and ought to rise up against him. By uniting their forces to chastise the common enemy. They shall discharge their duty towards themselves, and towards human society.

Everyone is at liberty to renounce his right, a state may acquire exclusive rights of navigation and fishing, by treaties. In which other states renounce in its favor the rights they derive from nature. The latter are obliged to observe their treaties; and the state they have favored has a right to maintain by force the possession of its advantages.

The rights of navigation and of fishing, and all other rights which may be exercised on the sea. Belong to the class of those rights of mere ability, which are imperceptible, they cannot be lost for want of use. Although a state should happen to have been, from time immemorial, in sole possession of the navigation or fishery in certain seas. It cannot claim an exclusive right to those advantages. Others shall not make use of their common right to navigation and fishery in those seas. It does not follow that they have had any intention to renounce it. They are entitled to exert it whenever they think proper.

The non-usage of the right may assume the nature of a consent or tacit agreement. Which become a title in favor of one state against another. When a state that is in possession of the navigation and fishery in certain tracts of sea claims an exclusive right to them and forbids all participation on the part of other nations. The others obey that prohibition with sufficient marks of acquiescence. They tacitly renounce their own right in favor of that state. Which establishes for it a new right, which they may afterwards lawfully maintain, especially when it is confirmed by long use.

The various uses of the sea near the coasts render it very susceptible of property. It furnishes fish, shells, pearls, amber and other natural resources. In all these respects, its use is not inexhaustible. The state to whom the coasts belong, may appropriate to themselves, and convert to their own profit, an advantage which nature has so placed within their reach as to enable them conveniently to take possession of it. In the same manner as they possessed themselves of the dominion of the land they inhabit. Where the catching of fish is the only object, the fishery appeals less liable to be exhausted. If a state has on their coast a particular fishery of a profitable nature, and of which they may become masters, shall they not be permitted to appropriate to themselves that bounteous gift of nature. An appendage to the land they possess, and to reserve to themselves the great advantages which their commerce may then derive in case there be a sufficient abundance of fish to furnish the neighboring states? If so far from taking possession of it, the state has acknowledged the common right of other states to come and fish there. It cannot exclude them from it. It has left that fishery in its primitive freedom, at least with respect to those who have been accustomed to take advantage of it.

A state may appropriate to itself those things of which the free and common use would be prejudicial or dangerous to it. This is a second reason for which governments extend their dominion over the sea along their coasts as far as they are able to protect their right. It is of considerable importance to the safety and welfare of the state that a general liberty is not allowed to all comers to approach so near their possessions. Especially with ships of war, as to hinder the approach of trading states, and molest their navigation parts of the sea subject to a state, are comprehended in its territory, must any one navigate them without its consent. Vessels that are not liable to suspicion the state cannot without a breach of duty, refuse permission to approach for harmless purposes. Since it is a duty incumbent on every proprietor to allow to strangers a free passage, even by land, when it may be done without damage or danger. It is true that the state itself is the judge of what is proper to be done in every particular case that occurs. If it judges amiss, it is to blame, but the others are bound to submit.

It is easy to determine to what distance a state may extend its rights over the sea by which it is surrounded. According to the common right of all states that border the sea, the dominion extends to the distance of twelve nautical miles from the coast. Each state may make what regulation it pleases so far as respects the transactions of the subjects with each other, or their concerns with the sovereign. The dominion of the state over the neighboring sea extends as far as its safety renders it necessary, and its power is able to assert it. A state cannot appropriate to itself a thing that is common to all mankind. Such as the sea, except so far as it has need of it for some lawful end. It would be a vain and ridiculous pretension to claim a right which it would be unable to assert. To establish a right of such extent, it is necessary to prove very clearly the express or tacit consent of all the powers concerned. Such pretensions are respected as long as the state that makes them is able to assert them by force.

The shores of the sea incontestably belong to the state that possesses the land of which they are a part. Ports and harbors are manifestly an appendage to and even a part of the land, and consequently are the property of the state. Whatever is said of the land itself will equally apply to them, so far as respects the consequences of the domain and of the state.

With regards to straits when they serve for a communication between two seas, the navigation of which is common to all, or several states. The state which possesses the strait cannot refuse the others a passage through it. Provided that passage be innocent and attended with no danger. By refusing it without just reasons, it would deprive those states of an advantage granted them by nature. The right to such a passage is a remnant of the primitive liberty enjoyed by all mankind. Nothing but the care of his own safety can authorize the owner of the strait to make use of certain precautions, and to require certain formalities. He has a right to levy a moderate tax on the vessels that pass, partly on account of the inconvenience they give him, by obliging him to be on his guard. As a return for the safety he procures them by protecting them from their enemies, by keeping pirates at a distance, and by defraying the expense attendant on the support of light-houses, sea-marks, and other things necessary to the safety of mariners.

If a sea is entirely enclosed by the territories of a state and has no other communication with the ocean than by a channel of which that state may take possession. Such a sea is no less capable of being occupied, and becoming property, than the land. It ought to follow the state of the land that surrounds it.

When a state takes possession of certain parts of the sea, it takes possession of the empire over them, as well as of the domain. These parts of the sea are within the jurisdiction of the state, and a part of its territory. The sovereign commands there, he makes laws, and may punish those who violate them. The king has the same rights there as on land, and in general, every right which the laws of the state allow him.

A state may possess the domain or property of a tract of land or sea, without having the sovereignty of it. It likewise happens that it shall possess the sovereignty of a place, of which the property, with respect to use, belongs to some other state. When a state possesses the useful domain of any place whatsoever, who has also the higher domain, or the sovereignty. One cannot from the possession of the state, infer with equal probability, a coexistent possession of the useful domain.

A state may have good reasons for claiming the land, and particularly over a tract of sea. Without pretending to have any property in it, or any   useful   domain.